EXPERTS
&
INFLUENCERS

WOMEN'S EMPOWERMENT

REBECCA HALL GRUYTER, COMPILER
#1 INTERNATIONAL BEST SELLING AUTHOR

Published 2020

Printed in the United States of America

Print ISBN: 978-1-7328885-8-6

Publisher Information:

RHG Media Productions

25495 Southwick Drive #103

Hayward, CA 94544

www.YourPurposeDrivenPractice.com

ACKNOWLEDGEMENTS

When writing an anthology, it takes many voices willing to join together to bring forth the book in a powerful and united way. It has been such an honor and privilege to work with this amazing group of Experts & Influencers. I want to thank these amazing leaders for entrusting us to bring forth and share their powerful stories.

I want to thank my husband for always cheering me on and encouraging me to SHINE! I thank God for giving me opportunities, opening doors, and bringing together the right people for this powerful project. I thank my parents for their love and support and my grandmothers for planting the legacy seeds to always choose to Bloom Where You Are Planted, Step Forward, and SHINE!

CONTENTS

FOREWORD

"EXPERTS & INFLUENCERS SERIES: WOMEN'S EMPOWERMENT EDITION"

BY REBECCA HALL GRUYTER, BOOK COMPILER

Thank you for leaning into this powerful anthology! I'm honored and excited to bring this powerful book featuring 15 experts that are committed to helping you be fully empowered to **SHINE**! Our vision is to have our experts and influencers share insights, tips, tools, and wisdom in the area of women's empowerment to support you on your journey to live an empowered and purpose filled life. We know life is not a solo journey and by coming together our goal is to help you step further into and more powerfully into your gifts, talents, and abilities as women. Together, as we lift each other up, we are all able to grow, reach more people, and have a greater impact.

In each chapter, our authors (all empowered women who are experts and influencers) will equip and empower you to more fully step forward with confidence and purpose. I believe this book is a living and interactive book that will speak wisdom, encouragement, and power into your life. I want to invite you to pause, take a deep breath, and be ready to receive these powerful chapters so they can ignite a fire in you, inspire courage in you, and help you to step fully into all that you are called to be.

We each need others to encourage us, to speak wisdom and truth to us, to love us and cheer us on, and to help us stand up again when we fall. This book will walk beside you to help you run and not grow weary, to complete all that you are called to complete, and to live on purpose and with great purpose while stepping more fully and powerfully into your calling.

In creating this book, I asked each expert and influencer to share a chapter that includes their wisdom, tips, and insights to support you as a woman. We asked them to share what they wished they would have known, what they have learned, and their best tips and insights to support you on your journey. Throughout the chapters you will feel a consistent and transparent heartbeat to support you in very real ways as the authors share authentically and powerfully from the heart. We want to make your journey easier for you to step forward and **SHINE**! As the book compiler, I'm so proud of what each co-author has shared in her chapter and am honored to have each of them leaning in to support you. I am equally honored that you have said "yes" to our book and are entrusting us to support you on your journey.

Now it's your turn. Are you going to lean in and learn from the wisdom within this book? Will you let us walk beside you on your journey of life? We want to lift you up, support you, encourage you, and empower you. It is your choice. You can choose to open the pages and let them pour into you, or you can put this book on a shelf. My heart and prayer are that you will say "yes" to you and lean into the powerful messages that are waiting to pour into you, your heart, and your life.

Here is how to get the most out of this powerful book. The book is divided into three sections, each one designed to meet you exactly where you are and to support you each step of your journey. **In the first section, Discover Your Power,** we help you discover and claim your power. **In the second section, Stand in Your Power,** our experts share how to stand in your gifts and talents and choose to live in a positive and empowered way. **In the third section, Own Your Power & SHINE!** Our authors share how to step forward (take action) in an empowered way and share the gift of you powerfully in the world. At the end of each powerful chapter, you will find the author's bio and contact information. I encourage you to "friend" and follow those authors with whom you feel a powerful resonance and connection so that they can continue to pour into you and support you on your journey in life.

****Special Augmented Reality Print Book Feature.**** We are excited to share that we have added the powerful cutting-edge REVEALiO technology to the print version of our book. You can download the free app and then once it's uploaded on your smart device, it will help the book cover come alive. After you download the free app onto your smart device, simply open the app and place the window over the cover of the book and a video message from us will start to play. A few of the authors in this book have also added a special video message to you, too. So, make sure to open the app and use it in the beginning of each chapter (putting the picture and title of the author's chapter in the screen box) and those that have saved a video message for you will immediately start playing. Enjoy this special feature and personal messages from our powerful authors.

Now the next step is yours. Drink-in the insights, tips, and wisdom that are within these pages to serve, support, and inspire you. Take the time to pause, read, and reflect. Listen to the powerful messages of hope that are waiting for you within the pages of this book. It's not an accident that you purchased this book and are opening it to read. I invite you to lean in and truly receive the messages and wisdom that will speak to your heart and soul that you will find in these transformational and dynamic pages. Enjoy this rich collection of wisdom, insight, and encouragement being provided by our amazing Experts & Influencers. We can't wait to see you SHINE!

-----Rebecca Hall Gruyter, Book Compiler
Founder/Owner of Your Purpose Driven Practice and CEO of RHG Media Productions

Rebecca Hall Gruyter

Rebecca Hall Gruyter is an Influencer and Empowerment Leader committed to bringing Experts and Influencers forward so that together we can lean in and make the world a better place one heart and life at a time. She is the owner of *Your Purpose Driven Practice*, creator of the *Women's Empowerment Series* events/TV show, the *Speaker Talent Search™*, and *Your Success Formula™*. Rebecca is an in-demand speaker, an expert money coach, and a frequent guest expert on success panels, tele-summits, TV, and radio shows. Rebecca specializes in using her promotional reach of over 10 million to help you be seen, heard, and SHINE!

As the CEO of RHG *Media Productions™*, Rebecca launched the international TV Network (www.RHGTVNetwork.com) to bring even more positive and transformational programming to the world. In July 2017, she launched the Global RHG Magazine bringing inspirational influencers to the world and their messages! In January 2018, she expanded RHG Publishing to now help individual authors bring their books forward as best sellers so they can be positioned as they bring their powerful books forward.

Rebecca is a popular and syndicated radio talk show host, #1 bestselling author (multiple times), and publisher who wants to help YOU impact the world powerfully!

Rebecca@YourPurposeDrivenPractice.com
www.facebook.com/rhallgruyter (Facebook)
www.YourPurposeDrivenPractice.com (Main Website)
www.RHGTVNetwork.com (TV Network)
www.SpeakerTalentSearch.com (Free Opportunity for Speakers to get on More Stages)
www.EmpoweringWomenTransformingLives.com (Weekly Radio Show)
www.MeetWithRebecca.com (Calendar link to schedule a time to talk with Rebecca)

SECTION 1:

Discover Your Power

CLAIMING YOUR SELF WORTH: A RITE OF PASSAGE
BY TINA M. DOWDY

It was a sunny day in June 1978 that marked the end of that horrible elementary school chapter of my life. The day one of the coolest boys I knew made a very profound and prophetic statement on my behalf to all of the 'mean girls.' He exclaimed that when we all move up to middle school in the fall, all the boys will want to date me over them because I was prettier! I stood there feeling just as stunned as those nasty little girls. His words made me feel so validated in that moment. Finally, someone sees me!

His name was John. It was the last day of school and I never saw him again. He spoke his truth and truth be told, **I honestly was a pretty young girl. The problem was that I never believed it. I was bullied and teased, and I didn't have a strong support system at home to build my self-esteem** or encourage the above-average grades that my sixth-grade teacher discovered I was capable of achieving. The seventh grade seemed so promising to me and graduation day couldn't arrive fast enough.

I grew up in Long Island, New York, a first generation Italian daughter and the youngest of six girls. **Like many little girls, I just did what I was told. We females have come to know this as being good little girls, which**

usually meant to be quiet or be agreeable; I was both. I found it difficult to express myself in such a large family and not having a voice felt very stifling and unnatural to me.

Most times I was just struggling to fit in, both at home and at school. I was a child swimming in a world of criticism, judgment and, often times, other people's chaos and conflict. **I grew to perceive my outer world as hostile and it made me feel very unsafe inside. I developed a witty sarcasm and kneejerk reaction to defend myself as I silently suffered with that loud and repetitive mantra in my mind "why don't they like me?"**

It wasn't always bad. There were times I felt safe to come up for air and I really loved those moments. Those points of validation where I would win a spelling bee, being chosen to be lead singer in school plays, cooking delish meals with my Mom's friend, dancing in the basement with my sister, or that one time when a boy named John said I was pretty. I felt little sparks of joy in my heart that gave me hope.

I was too young and misguided to be clear on what was most meaningful to me in life. I felt lost and unloved, so I did what any good little girl would do—I made other people happy. I sought out praise from any willing adult who would occasionally see me in my goodness. Those split seconds of approval brought out the best in me. It became an addiction that my inner child carried into my adulthood.

I have discovered that the limiting beliefs we have today are developed in our childhood. The conditioning of our upbringing, the traditions of our ancestral background, and the roles other people play in our lives is how we, as children, perceive our own position within our tribe. The opinions we form, about ourselves and others, begin right here, and the voids we try to fill within ourselves will determine how we make choices as adults. **In short, your inner five year old has already decided your significance in life more than you know.**

I grew into a young woman that would repeatedly put others needs before my own. To see a boss rate my job performance review as "exceeds expectations" or a boyfriend say "you're so beautiful" would feel like it gave my soul a glimpse of what it was like to feel free from the suffocation of criticism, guilt, and shame. The brief moments I felt confident and my inner expression whispered "I am worthy".

I became very outgoing, well-travelled, competitive and overly accommodating in both my personal and professional lives. **My outer world perceived me as highly competent, yet my inner voice kept pushing me to feel complete. I was blindsided by my ego; nothing ever seemed to be good enough.** I ended up doing more and more to prove myself, and my daily rhythm became very fast paced to get it all done.

I was trying to achieve perfection. **My first panic attack snuck up on me one morning on my commute to Manhattan. I was 29,** my heart palpitations were out of control, my legs were numb, and the two minute train ride to get off the next stop felt like hours of hell. This was my wake up call.

That uncontrollable feeling of anxiety was my body's way of forcing me to slow down and pause so that it could bring to my attention that I was stressing myself out. I was pushing myself to unhealthy levels and neglecting my own self-care! It was my soul's way of screaming, "STOP running in circles! You're missing the whole point! It's about self-love!"

I began to dabble in mindfulness practices with a mentor, which motivated me to go back to college to be a wellness practitioner. I took two years of Tai Chi and I made an effort to apply as many mind, body, and spirit principles into my own life so I could feel balanced. I graduated with awards and a better sense of self, but apparently, my newfound knowledge of the human anatomy and meditation was only the beginning.

I was 32 when I first started working for myself, and by age 36 I opened up my first therapeutic spa and yoga studio. Little did I know that I just signed myself up for the toughest lessons in leadership that would reveal my most defining moments of self-worth. Owning a business is not for the faint of heart. It will fully expose your sense of self, your coping skills, the people you attract and the habits you bring to it as a result of a scarcity mindset.

In spite of all I learned, I was oblivious that my insecurities were still calling the shots for me, and so my ambitious ego still wanted to conquer the world. I would soon learn that not even the highest of aspirations or the smartest of minds stood a fair chance when the sneaky voice of the inner critic was given too much authority to articulate itself. Like most women that age, I thought I had it all under control.

Even when you follow all the rules, good intentions will go really bad when the voice of your inner goddess is being muted. After all, she is your fearless leader that empowers you to learn the elemental laws of success. She is the part of you that summons the courage to be authentic, vulnerable, and rooted in your core values so that every decision you make comes from that space of self-realization. It was time for me to open my heart to her.

If you want to be your own boss, then develop actual leadership skills with which to lead yourself. Allow me to save you some valuable time and energy here. Even if you graduated with the highest of honors, **you cannot attain the leadership attributes of a strong inner goddess unless you begin with these two processes: to *develop a strong sense of self-awareness and to retain a trusted mentor that will show you how.***

A life that feels tangled in chaos and conflict is a tell-tale sign that you are allowing your insecurities to run the show. You ignore all the red flags, which means you are betraying your own intuition. The whole 'fake it until you make' theory does not work because it only intensifies your self-doubt. You will end up settling for unhealthy relationships and financial scenarios that do not serve your highest and greatest good.

Giving other people the power to confirm your worthiness is guaranteed to disappoint you. Your competency and reliability to carry out a job does not secure financial growth, and your physical beauty will never guarantee that you won't end up with a narcissistic spouse that uses you for your loving and sensual touch while they leave you hanging and unsatisfied, cheat on you, or abuse you.

What I know for sure is that if self worth is one of your life lessons, then you will find yourself spinning your wheels over and over again with toxic issues until you discover your true value. Your body will warn you that your constant feelings of despair and anxiety will spiral you to crash and burn. For many women, this becomes the defining moment of change. When your world collides and you become sick and tired of being sick and tired. This is the opportunity for growth.

The more you practice this inner work of awareness, the more you will identify what deeply motivates you so you can uncover and conquer your triggers, react less, and problem solve more. Being solution-focused is an attribute of a strong emotional IQ—it encompasses the qualities, coping skills and habits of a true leader. Whether you're leading a tribe or just leading yourself, you must develop a strong emotional intelligence to succeed. You're sense of worth depends on it.

The truth is the most soulful and accomplished people I know learned that great strength comes in being vulnerable. Just like a new job, if you are learning to do something new, then you must be guided by someone who has already been there.

When you are self aware, you are mindful of your thoughts and actions so you can learn how to make choices in life from a place of authenticity and worthiness.

Another bonus of self awareness is that it activates and strengthens your intuition. We are all born with this inner navigator that our left brain loves to ignore. When you know how your intuition works, you will be able to confidently steer your direction in life.

I highly encourage you to meditate. If your mind is very busy, it is best to start with a guided meditation that instructs you on what to do. To get you started, I have composed a complimentary self-worth meditation for you that you can retrieve on my website at: www.tinadowdy.com.

Anything worth having can only manifest from believing that you are worthy of it. We all want to matter, but no one will respect you more than you give them permission to. **If you truly want to be happy, then it's time to take responsibility by communicating healthy boundaries in your relationships, and it starts with the relationship you have with yourself.**

Claiming your self-worth means developing strong spiritual muscles:

It starts with one simple concept: ***begin by giving people their dignity***.

This uncomplicated and profound piece of advice came from a lovely man named Ken that I met in Tampa when I attended Kevin Harrington's Pitch Tank Workshop. Ken is a very successful and soulful entrepreneur and was soon to be an author. One night, I decided to sit with him and his amazing young son at the hotel restaurant and we were having this delightful conversation on the topic of spirituality. I was in a place in time where I was feeling a bit lost and questioning my life purpose, and so I told Ken that I was seeking the guidance of a spiritual mentor, but I wasn't sure how to find one.

His sincere response was, "*First practice giving people their dignity, then your teacher will show up*." I was inspired and instinctively compelled to listen this very gracious and accomplished man who made space at his dinner table for me. He was in my life for what seemed like a split second and I am so grateful I took heed of his advice.

Opportunities began to show up for me along the way, and I seized them to learn as much as I could from many different teachers on how to master my own mind and still be aligned to my heart. In retrospect, I realize that it is within this crucial step that determines if the student is ready for the teacher.

I learned that deliberately giving people their dignity is a conscious act of kindness that literally forces you to filter your thoughts before you say something to someone. It was an act of self-awareness.

It opens this pathway in your mind that makes you take a step back and pause to hear the unwitting voice of your inner critic and judge—the voice of shame and guilt that accuses people of not being smart or physically attractive enough or worthy of being loved.

It gives you backstage access to the part of your mind that diminishes people of their worth and makes you conscious of it. You will be astounded at how many disapproving thoughts you really have about people.

This inner bully part of the human mind exists in all of us. It does not matter whether you are saying horrible things to people or just thinking them because your negative beliefs about others only mirror those same exact soul-crushing insecurities you've had about yourself all along. This is where your most powerful self-worth breakthrough begins.

It's the moment you realize your potential is much more than what you've become and you now have the ability to make an informed decision to remedy it by doing something different.

Self-worth is not something you're born with—it's a rite of passage. It's the moment in time when you decide to stop chasing that imaginary ladder of success that our culture has conditioned us to climb and you stop buying into the make believe rules to be physically, mentally, and financially perfect. **When you can embrace being perfectly imperfect, then you will know you have arrived at a very magical place inside yourself.**

The real secret to success is when you've mastered the wisdom to feel worthy inside. It's when you're clear on your core values and you trust the decisions you make in life because they are aligned to those values. **It's when your sense of belonging in this world trumps your need to fit in because you finally realize that no one has the power to make you feel marvelous or miserable unless you let them.**

When you are able to create your own meaningful definition of success, then you have arrived at a place of self acceptance, forgiveness and trust in yourself. Self-care becomes a priority because you've learned self-love. You understand your worthiness, and it's from this place that you can speak blessings into yourself and unto others. You radiate light, and from this place miracles will happen and there is no going back to where you once were.

Claim Your Self Worth

1. Develop a daily practice to build your self-awareness (meditating, journaling, allowing yourself to listen to your thoughts and feelings).
2. Choose to give people their dignity and treat them with respect and kindness.
3. Build your emotional I.Q.
4. Look for mentors and coaches that can support you on your journey.
5. Remember, no one can make you feel marvelous or miserable unless you let them.
6. Embrace self-love and self-care.
7. Claim and stand for your self-worth..

Tina Dowdy

With over 21 years of experience and success as a health professional and entrepreneur, I help smart and soulful women professionals, like you, to take the fear of failure out of business planning and gain clarity to achieve your next levels of income and ignite your joy factor!

I have made it my mission in life to guide you on how to safely navigate your next steps to thrive in your profession in a way that keeps you authentic, with your heart fully open to be seen, heard, supported, and valued in all of your brilliance and worth as woman!

With numerous credentials, training, and achievements in meditation, intuitive counseling, hypnosis, leading workshops, and business coaching, the work I do today reflects the exact assistance I needed to sustain me in my first wellness business in 1998: *support that is rooted in accountability, non-judgment, putting profitable systems into place, managing self-care to prevent burnout, and helping you to keep things real.*

I am a spirited entrepreneur that enjoys supporting women to successfully leave their legacy. I use a proven customized model that integrates business strategy with mindful approaches that will take you beyond your survival skills, exceed the knowledge of your craft, and take you further than a great business plan.

My two biggest lessons as a woman entrepreneur are (1) *women thrive best when they are supported* and (2) *your personal growth will totally determine your business growth*!

www.tinadowdy.com

BE A CHANGE AGENT!!
BY PAULA OREZI

My life's motto is to be a change agent in everything I do! The good thing about life is that you have each day to regroup and focus on the mission of living life to the fullest! Jokingly, I would say, "*I don't do normal.*" The meaning of this is that **I do not see life as being ordered and normal; instead, I see life as an adventure filled with plots and twists that feels like a crazy ride at a theme park!** I believe that becoming a change agent is the foundation for real positive impact to start occurring in communities. **As an influencer, my life's mission is to help others to be influencers on a smaller scale, to branch out and create this positive change.** Creating influencers to influence!

When I look around me, the "normal" life includes doing things as we are taught to do, such as following the traditions of life (school, working, marriage, children). There is a ladder of success that everyone is trying to climb. **I am a firm believer that everyone has their own path in life. What gets us in trouble is when we try to follow other people and their life's path.** We all have our own unique life story that can add to the big puzzle of LIFE. We create our own destiny with our choices. I don't like following the "normal" route that everyone takes. I am accepting who I am and know that I have my own life path. If I step off of my path, then I will lose myself and get caught up in someone else's path. I want to find my path and way to access success in life. **The best thing is to accept my path of life and be myself!** Those who do normal get normal things. I want to exceed in all I do. No more cookie cutter life for me!

However, I didn't always feel this way. During my teen years, I struggled like the typical teenager with self-identity and worth. I grew up in a strict home. I thought of myself as not being good enough to be someone important in life or to offer anything of value to others. **I quickly started to doubt my existence in this world.** My thinking had an impact on my decisions in life. **I used to compare myself to others, thinking if I only had their gifts, talents, and abilities, then I could bring something valuable to the table. I quickly learned that I was stuck with *Me* for life and I needed to be okay with that!** During my years in college, I wanted to start my own business. I tried every business opportunity that came my way no matter the objectives. I had no clear idea what I was aiming for in life and I was lost!

Then I started my life in Corporate America and immediately became harder on myself because I felt so devalued and minimized. In every job that I had, I felt intimidated to take on new projects, give presentations, or lead others. I kept allowing outside influences in the workplace to define who I was and what my abilities were. I did not want to be rejected, so I would go with the flow.

After several jobs and setbacks of business opportunities, I realized that I had not defined my life's mission. Therefore, I would accept anything that came my way instead of taking a closer look to see if it fits who I am and what I stand for. **Going along with the flow was not what I wanted. One day during my time at work, my thinking changed**. I started to see myself as a person that can create change by simply being myself and being a change agent in everything I do. **I can actually choose to bring positive change to the world and get out of my comfort zone to help others have that defining moment as well.** I believe we are created for a purpose, for a time to be ourselves and contribute in this world using our gifts, talents, and abilities.

This new perspective led me to create a simple T-Shirt that stated that I am Good Enough! I developed it with the idea that sometimes staring at a T-shirt that has a statement is worth more than speaking it out loud. I used to be a shy person and now I have developed a confidence that allows me to use my talents to be expressive in creative ways. **The *Paula O! Store* was born!** It was birthed out of frustration of how the world has cookie-cutter standards on who a person should be, and I wanted to take a stand for all of us to be ourselves as an important piece to being a change agent.

The name of the blog was created to offer a place of motivation, learning, and community. My WHY is to help others not feel outcasted but to be themselves and let their talents display unashamed! The journey was hard and long, but the rewarding fact of it all is that I am living the best life today all because I stepped out of my comfort zone, developed a roadmap of goals, and connected with others that would invest in me to get to that destiny! I hope the life lessons I discovered on the way can help you on your journey.

<u>If I were a younger me, I would have shared some of these important tips that could have saved me from doing the normal routines of LIFE in the earlier years of my journey!</u>

- **<u>Everyone has a story to tell. What's your story?</u>** – Life experiences are meant to be shared to help others and your story matter since it is a part of this big thing called . . . LIFE! **Do not take your life for granted. No one had a roadmap to life. You are the owner of your life.** Developing a routine of journaling helps to outline each experience. Often review your journal entries a year later and you will gain a different perspective on each life experience. There is a constant cycle in life where we are all in a *temporary* season to prepare for the *greater* season! Think about all you went through in your personal life and career path. What were some valuable lessons that you would want to share to your younger self? Reflection is important in the process because it helps you to notice the smaller details and develop them into wisdom. Learn to stay in each moment and pause for a while and let the experiences have a conversation with you. Doing so helps develop a healthy relationship with yourself and how you share your story to others! No one has the first experience of your life but YOU!

- **<u>Next step towards your dreams</u>** – Think about your thoughts and daily investments (time, relationships, personal growth, money). Ask yourself these two important questions, "*What am I doing outside my comfort zone? What takes up my time?*" **Doing a daily assessment of making an account of how each hour is spent is crucial. What you invest in eventually grows!** Take the time at the end of each day to do a time evaluation and write down what you did for each hour of the day from waking up to going to bed. **Time is like money . . . we have to budget every single minute and where it goes.** What does the in-between look like? Stepping into a greater version of YOU requires self-discipline in how you invest your time and with whom. You plant seeds along life's journey, but what kind of seeds are you planting? **In your relationships, evaluate who you are around. Be around forward thinkers!** You need to find someone who will tag you along, not drag you along. Lesson to learn: ***there are dream -catchers and dream-chasers. Which one are you?***

- **<u>Be You</u>** - Get up and be YOU. **You are not a copy but an original and custom made to be part of the world's puzzle!** No one can do what you can do! People may have similar skills and talents, but no one can creatively articulate the talents the way you do. Love yourself enough to break up with being a copy image of someone else! Pop the dream bubble of, "*If I were only her or him,*" and start to accept the fact that YOU are here and YOU are all you've got to imprint something meaningful to this world. What does it mean to be YOU? Ask yourself, "*What part of YOU did you leave behind in order to be someone else?*" People tend to focus on the results of what others are achieving but fail to realize that the results derive from the fact that they were themselves. **Be okay with who YOU were meant to be. It is fun to discover your gifts and talents by paying attention to yourself daily.** What do you find yourself doing the most? What makes you happy when you do it? What keeps you curious? **This is a good start to learn to love yourself and the journey!**

Creating influencers to influence is all tied to being a change agent. No one person can do it all! Developing daily habits with insightful tips can be a motivation to be empowered to take a leap of faith and to stop being the "*normal*" person! Once you change your perspective on small thinking patterns, it can open your eyes to a greater part of life! **Life is not a box with perfect edges and flaps. Life is meant to be discovered and appreciated**. The beginning and end has already been defined, but it is in the in-between that people lose their way. Focusing on the mission of your life is important because your life is a building block for the next generation.

As mentioned earlier, my life's motto is to be a change agent in everything I do because everything I do daily matters and each experience in my life matters. I often create a think tank session with myself at my favorite coffee shop. I reflect on decisions that I have to make and then write down what would be a roadblock for each action that I need to take.

What about you? What is your life's motto? What will you commit to doing today to be a change agent? Some decisions require bold steps. It all starts with knowing that you have a life story that you are the author of, creating next steps towards your dreams, and being your authentic self while discovering all that life has to offer! **Take the adventure** and discover a step into your purpose. Share more of you!

Paula Orezi

Paula Orezi is the author of a motivational poetry book titled *From Me to You*. She was born in Allentown, Pennsylvania and was raised in South Florida. She earned a Master's in Business Leadership from Huizenga School of Business at Nova Southeastern University and a Bachelor's degree in Organizational Management from Palm Beach Atlantic University. She has a passion to speak and help people get inspired to make a change that will create a positive and win-win outcome. Her experience includes mentoring others and leadership development. Paula's life motto is to be a change agent in everything she does. Her messages are for business-minded professionals or anyone wishing to start their own business and need help to overcome mindset beliefs, being organized, and conducting sales through relationship-building. These are the ingredients that she believes others can benefit from to see results. Paula's WHY is to help people overcome destructive patterns regarding thinking habits and daily investment habits. Paula has been featured in podcasts that encourage others to live with purpose and dream BIG! The creation of the Paula O! Store was founded on the concept of *Be You!* She has impacted many with her branded products that stand for the mission of empowering others to be themselves and find their life's calling in an adventurous way.

Paula Orezi, *Author & Speaker*
Paula O! Store
Personal email: porez815@gmail.com
Business email: info@paulaostore.com
Phone: (754) 333-1623
Website: www.paulaostore.com
Facebook: @paulaostore
Instagram: @paulaostore

BECOMING EXTRAORDINARY – LIVING LIFE WITH PURPOSE

BY MICHELLE CALLOWAY

I used to hide behind my mom's dress when someone would talk to me as a child. In adolescence, beauty did not become me as it did my older sister. My hair was thin and stringy, I wore big-rimmed glasses in gold metal frames, and my uneven front teeth made for an awkward and uncomfortable smile.

Cupid's arrow struck me early in life, though. At age fourteen, I fell in love with a handsome boy who was four years older than me. I didn't feel worthy or lovely at that point in my life, so I didn't really expect much to happen in that regard. As it turns out, I underestimated myself and what other people thought of me. Who knew?! Evidently, this young man saw through the stringy hair, thick glasses, and jagged teeth and saw me, the real me. **He liked the real me and we became very good friends. Our friendship blossomed into romance and I married my best friend when I was only 19 years old.**

Through the process of learning to love him, he helped me learn how to love myself, or at least begin to. I had a real problem accepting

compliments. Can you relate at all? When someone would say something complimentary to me, I would shrug it off and half-heartedly say "Thank You." I wasn't able to accept it in my heart.

My husband helped me overcome my inferiority complex by sharing how hurtful it was to him when I behaved like this. He would (authentically) compliment me on how beautiful he thought I was, only to witness me roll my eyes and dismiss the compliment. He was tired of me belittling myself and sternly told me so. Never had I seen him so upset! He shouted, "Start learning how to take a compliment! You're beautiful to me and I love you! It hurts me when you don't believe what I'm saying to you!"

Wow, huh?! I never really thought that my inability to accept a compliment would have a negative effect on others. Have you ever felt unworthy, unlovely, or unbecoming? It has taken me decades to fully be able to accept compliments without cringing a little on the inside. **What really helped me overcome my inferiority complex was finding my faith and my purpose.**

Purpose

"I believe there's a calling for all of us. I know that every human being has value and purpose. The real work of our lives is to become aware. And awakened. To answer the call."
–Oprah Winfrey

We are all born with a God-given purpose. It's up to us to tap into a relationship with our creator in order to discover what that purpose is. Having faith in a higher power outside of your own self is incredibly liberating and allows you to live life on purpose, for a purpose, rather than merely existing.

Everyone comes into finding their life's purpose in different ways. You may experience an internal nudging, a vision, an audible voice inside your head, or a clear sign through something you see, read, or hear from someone else. Don't ignore the signs, however they may come to you. Take action! Step out of your comfort zone and begin your journey. **Stand firm in your faith knowing that you are on a path to fulfill your purpose in life, your destiny, nothing can derail you from this mission.**

My calling came in the form of a dream, and audible voice, a visit from an acquaintance, and another vision years later. I was being led to step beyond my profession of digital media and step into an unknown realm of emerging technology that would reshape my future and the lives of others. I am now a thought leader in the technology industry, and I lead a business community and host a TV show. It's crazy to look back and see where I've come from, but this calling is bigger than I am and it's fulfilling, even though it's scary at times.

Living your life with purpose breeds confidence that doesn't come from your outward beauty or presentation. It comes from your core. **Confidence comes more from who you are, what you stand for, and why you are doing what you are doing.** If you don't currently like yourself very much, promise yourself to start changing that narrative now. Work on becoming your biggest cheerleader.

Confidence is beautiful when it is accompanied with humility. Some people confuse confidence with arrogance. Be kind and courteous to others no matter how successful you become. The golden rule is to always treat others the way you would like to be treated.

As a woman leader, your confidence can and probably will intimidate or offend some men. Pray for those that falsely speak against you and remain true to your purpose. Grace and humility will help guard your heart, allowing you to move on from those instances with renewed purpose and confidence.

Don't go it alone. On my journey, I have found that it really strengthens my confidence when I surround myself with professional mentors. When I come to a fork in the road and need to make a big life-altering decision, I ask some of my mentors about it and weigh their responses before making a final decision. This process shores up my confidence and prevents undue pressure or anxiety over the situation. Do you have a mentor or two? If so, hold them close. They're absolutely invaluable.

Passion

"There is no passion to be found playing small—in settling for a life that is less than the one you are capable of living."
–Nelson Mandela

People tell me all the time that they love how passionate I am about what I do. I'm doing exactly what I am supposed to be doing and it feels amazing! How about you? Are you on fire for your purpose, your why?

Passion is a form of inspiration. When you are tapped into your purpose, your passion to fulfill that purpose becomes your fuel throughout your journey. Others will find your passion inspirational, and it may even lead them to join you on your journey. Others may be inspired by your willingness to step out of your comfort zone to fulfill your God-given purpose, that they too decide to take their first steps. Passion and inspiration have a ripple effect. You're already making a difference in people's lives. You're building a legacy. Well done!

Perseverance

"Faithfulness is only measured by faithfulness."
–Pastor Chris Brown

It's not always easy, in fact you might find that living your life on purpose is actually very hard work. It's the most gratifying kind of work I've ever experienced, though. Knowing you are doing exactly what you are supposed to be doing drives you to keep showing up every day, no matter what.

If you like to be in control, I highly recommend you loosen the reigns and let God lead you on your journey. The reality is that none of us are in full control of our lives. We are only able to control our choices and our behavior. Begin trusting your purpose for existence. Trust in God that you are fulfilling your divine purpose, and that He has your back. He knows what is best for you, and He will guide you every step of the way.

Don't ever give up! Your journey's path may not always look the way you expected it to. You may go through more valleys than peaks at times.

Remember you've been called for a purpose. Pay attention to whom you are becoming through the process. You are building character, grit, and resilience. You are becoming a better person for having said "yes" to your calling.

You will run into nay-sayers on your journey. In fact, sometimes it's the people closest to you that become toxic to your personal growth and development. **Not everyone will understand your purpose, and they may feel threatened by it.** Some people may feel that your purpose is taking you away from them.

I have had to level-up many times on my journey. What I mean is, I've had to purge and re-build my friendship circles to only include those that support and encouragement my efforts. **As You level-up, you'll desire to hang out with like-minded, driven, and successful people because they can relate to the struggle, hard work, and perseverance it takes to pursue your God-given purpose in life.**

By saying "yes" to your calling, you have essentially said "goodbye" to an ordinary life. Your calling is so much bigger than you, and your soul will not rest until you have done all that you can to fulfill your calling. You know you were meant for more, and there's no going back now. You were meant for an extraordinary and purpose filled life!

Enjoy the ride, stay open-minded, seek guidance from God and your mentors, never give up, stay true to your purpose, treat yourself well, rest often, pray often, laugh often, love graciously, be humble, be a good friend, serve others often, and you will become all that you were destined to be.

To your success,
Michelle

Living a Life with Purpose Tips:

1. Acknowledge that you were born with a purpose.
2. Open your heart and mind to discover your purpose.
3. Stand firm in your faith, mission, and purpose.
4. Stand confident in who you are called to be.
5. Level up. Hang out with supportive people who inspire you to want to continually better yourself.
6. Bring your passion and energy to what you choose to do.
7. Don't ever give up! Remember you are called for a purpose.
8. Commit to being "ALL IN" and experience your best, most extraordinary life!

Michelle Calloway

Michelle Calloway is an International Speaker, Bestselling Author and CEO of an innovative software solutions company called REVEALiO.

REVEALiO serves the emerging world of augmented reality (or AR), which reveals virtual content when real-world objects or images are viewed through a mobile or wearable smart device. This interactive experience has shown to increase engagement and conversions exponentially.

Michelle has been featured in Inc. Magazine, and praised by Kevin Harrington, of ABC's Hit TV Show, Shark Tank, for providing small business owners with a unique differentiator that creates powerful organic conversions.

She is driven by success and determined to help forward-thinking businesses gain the ultimate competitive advantage by captivating their audiences and influencing buying decisions with interactive branded experiences.

REVEALiO, has now made AR and the interactive branded experience accessible and affordable to everyone. Michelle says "these interactions enhance human connection and empower business owners to have more impact, influence, and income".

Michelle is also Founder of the Tech with Heart Network, an online business community and TV show. Her Tech with Heart Network further empowers small business owners to achieve rapid success, leveraging the power of media exposure and celebrity status. The power of this network can take a new business owner with no pre-existing track record and create instant credibility in any market.

Email: mcalloway@revealio.com
Websites:
https://revealio.com
https://techwithheartnetwork.com
https://michellecalloway.us

WOMEN AND CLEAR COMMUNICATION FIND YOUR VOICE, USE YOUR SUPERPOWERS

BY JEANNE ALFORD

We speak. Are you sure we are speaking to each other?

We tweet. We Facebook. We Instagram. We Pinterest. We Periscope. We text. Do we get to be heard for who we really are?

We live by email. Is it effective?

We whisper. We shout. Are we heard?

I can tell you truthfully, that many times in my career, I had my doubts. Knowing how to communicate and deliver information clearly, concisely and directly is critical. Knowing how that information is received is priceless.

For women, however, you need to add "how" to that list. It's that old saw about the difference between being assertive and being aggressive. Knowing "how" that information is received is priceless.

We are judged differently. We are expected to take everyone's feelings into consideration and be diplomatic. One of my bosses accused me of being aggressive when I delivered a presentation. I was too forceful in his eyes. I learned to be deliberate in my presentations and talks but be mindful of the audience. I found that to be heard, I had to gauge the audience—what are they most interested in? How can I reach them?

We have more ways to "communicate" on more and more platforms. **The secret is in the message, not the medium or the platform.**

Canadian philosopher Marshal McLuhan, back in the mid-1960's, famously declared that the "medium is the message." His intent, to declare that the medium influenced the form of human interactions. Keep in mind, however, in the mid-1960s in the U.S., we had three major television networks, a few local stations, newspapers, radio stations and the movies. Compared to the number of media outlets today, this is but a drop in the ocean.

With everything at our fingertips, it's time to reconsider McLuhan's thesis and declare the "message is the medium." By this, I mean the content we send through our various platforms are critical to ensure we are heard.

In this chapter, I will explore a few key points in finding and using your voice, ensuring that your message can be heard.

Beyond Simply Speaking: A Deliberate Choice

Someone speaks. You answer.

Did you immediately answer, or did you take a moment, a breath, to hear what was said and fashion an appropriate response? For many of us, we want to add context and history. The result? Our message is lost. It's important to focus on the most important points.

Did you know that we stop hearing our conversation partner before they are finished? Our mind switches into a response-finding mode, looking for that pearl of wisdom that can prove how smart or clever we are.

It takes a skill to slow your mind and hear the whole sentence. It takes practice. It takes repeating what you heard. For example, how many times have you responded with, "I think I heard you say . . . ?"

By fully hearing your conversation partner's information and taking a moment to process it, you can ensure you answer with your message. Sounds easy, right? Try it out. You will be surprised that you need to exercise some brain neurons that you didn't even know you had!

The Power of Communications

I did a workshop recently on the power of communications. I stood in front of the group and asked, "Do you talk?" The audience chuckled as they raised their hands. One bright executive said a bit louder than she wanted, "Of course and often too much." (More giggles emanated.)

I waited a beat, then I asked, "Do you communicate?"

This time only a few hands tentatively raised, but I noted some questioning looks. I followed with, "Do you know the difference?"

Talk is a big term with lots of meanings—a speech, a lesson in a classroom, an activity between two people and so on. But communications, at its base, is an exchange of information. When McLuhan was opining about the medium being the message, he had TV, radio, newspaper and cinema to consider. These support one-way transmission of content to an audience. A one-to-many communications model.

With social media, like Facebook, Twitter and so forth, we now have a two-way platform that allows you to send information out. Your followers have an opportunity to respond. However, many continue to use these platforms as if they are a one-to-many model.

The One-on-One Experience

Your audience, whether a single person or a larger group, makes their first judgment of you in the first two and a half seconds. How? We exhibit micro expressions, according to Forbes Magazine, that communicate a lot of information. Consider, do you stand straight or do you have a slight shoulder slump?

In a profile in AdWeek, advertisers, like Coca Cola, report that we have five seconds to capture someone's attention beyond our micro expressions. I knew it was a fast response, but five seconds? Watch today's commercials and search for the "hook" to keep you engaged. You'll find it in the first 12 words.

What this means to us is simple. If we are not focused on what is important to our audience—whether it's a colleague or friend, an email recipient or a customer far away—we need to capture their attention quickly.

Why is this important to know?

We live in a world of overwhelming information. To get your message across, you need to capture your audience's attention and provide information that is important to them.

The World of Overwhelm

For many of us, we see the world is speeding up. Things are moving faster and faster. Whether this is proved by physicists or debunked, it's a perception that we are on a fast hamster wheel we call life. It's true!

In his 1997 book, *Data Smog*, David Schenk points out that the information we get in one daily newspaper, like the New York Times, is equal to the amount of information a 17th century man would encounter in a lifetime. (Keep in mind that this was BEFORE Facebook, Twitter, et al.)

In 2010, University of California San Diego published a study that said we are exposed to 34 gigabytes of data daily. That's the equivalent of more than 100,000 words, the size of a Stephen King novel and more.

An industry magazine, Adweek, added that we get so much digital information sent to us that it's the equivalent of 1,000 clicks and seven hours of video.

Fun facts, right?

We get a Stephen King novel, 1,000 clicks and seven hours of video daily. No wonder we are overwhelmed.

Being aware of the amount of distraction we are buried under daily—plus our jobs, our families, our friends and ourselves—it's important to have tools to help manage our way through it all. I advocate using these "superpower tools" before you tweet, Facebook, chat, text, email, talk or call.

Conversation Superpowers: Breathe, Listen, Choose

In my last corporate position, my team presented me with one of those funny plaques to hang on my wall. It said, "Home of the Breathing Lady." For those who know me, they found it funny, because I was constantly saying, "Take a breath." Working on a deadline, "take a breath." In the midst of a crisis? "Take a breath." Running behind for meeting with the CEO? Yep, "take a breath."

I list breathing, listening and choosing as conversation superpowers.

Breathing, like riding a bike, is a muscle memory activity. We learned how to breathe when we left our mother's womb. We breathe in our upper lungs and get the oxygen to live. The breathing I advocate is deep breathing—cleansing breaths and such. Simply taking a breath moves your thought processing from the back of the brain in the fight-flight-freeze area to the logical frontal lobal. But more important, it gives you a nanosecond to, as my Dad used to tell me, **"engage brain before opening mouth."** Yeah, Dad was sarcastic but supportive.

Once you've got your thought process calm and ready, the next tool is **Listening**. I mentioned earlier that many of us, yes, I include myself in this esteemed group, often stop listening halfway through our conversation partner's statement. If you get a chance, listen to a few distracted people talking. It's illustrative. One says something about an event, the other jumps in with "I know, did you see that widget" and off they go on a huge tangent.

I use Family Feud as an example. Steve Harvey reads "according to 100 surveyed, the best room in the house to," and BAM. The contestant hits the buzzer. How can they know what to say? He could be looking for any room and the contestant is, no doubt, going to miss.

Practice listening all the way through. I realize that it may seem awkward, but that's simply because it's not something we do every day. When you practice this, it will become more like a muscle memory process like breathing and riding a bike. This skill, and it is a skill, will improve all your communications activities simply because you will have the right information.

The final communication superpower is the unsung hero, **Choosing**. Using the power to choose is critical in how you control or guide a situation, whether it's a one-on-one conversation or picking the right restaurant to meet your best friends. Choosing is the only power we have complete control over. Do we choose to react emotionally and "shoot from the hip?" or do we choose to reply by taking a breath, listening and choosing to respond thoughtfully and deliberately? For most of us, the latter is the best choice, but like breathing and listening, it's a skill that you might need to practice more so it too can become a muscle memory process.

By becoming more skillful at applying the Breathe, Listen, Choose tools, you can better navigate that noisy, distracting world we live in. You have something to say.

Communications Magic

You can change your world one conversation at a time by simply asking yourself a few questions. I'll say it here. With practice, you can do these questions in the span of those deep breaths you'll be taking.

What is this "communications magic?"

These questions are tools that help me to hone in to the most important information for someone—whether I'm giving a talk, conducting a workshop or speaking to my kids.

The first magic question: "What do I need to say?"

I mentioned earlier that we often stop hearing our conversation partner before they are done speaking. Another thing we often do is jump in without knowing what we really need to say. In my world, we refer to this as a "shoot from the hip" conversation. These tend to be reactionary and, often, not very focused or effective. When you take a moment and ask yourself what you need to say, you have a nanosecond to move the conversation the way you need it to go.

The next magic question: "Why is it important to them?"

I call this the empathy card. By taking a moment and realizing that most folks start from a "what's in it for me?" perspective, you can again guide the conversation to get the information you need. For example, if you are reporting to your boss on your budget, you know your boss cares about if your spending on schedule or not. You can then focus your conversation specifically.

The final magic question: "What action do I want to draw out?"

Stephen Covey wrote, "Begin with the end in mind." I find this advice priceless. I learned this as a negotiating tool in a sales workshop, too. So, let me point out, an effective conversation is often an effective negotiation. Knowing what you want to accomplish before you start the conversations helps to guide you in preparation and in sharing the right level of information with your conversation partner. The actions could be agreement to tasks like planning a dinner or as simple as identifying a decision to be made or a request to be aware of an issue.

Conversations can sometimes feel like a tug of war! You have something to say. Your partner has something else on their mind. Who's in charge? By using the Breathe, Listen and Choose tools, you can ensure your partner that you hear her. You can guide the conversation by being aware of what you need to say and what's important to your partner.

Changing the McLuhan philosophy that the medium is the message is a change of perception. Your message is as important as the media you use. I teach that communications is an art and a science. **The art is the what you have to say, the science is how you get it said. By getting into the habit of planning your communications—just three magic questions—you will see your communications muscles grow stronger and, I trust, your voice becomes clearer.**

Communication Tips

1. Remember to stop, pause and breathe.
2. Fully listen to the person speaking.
3. Then, choose your response.
4. Communication goes both ways.
5. Manage the overwhelm of information.
6. Be clear on your message.
7. Share your message.

Jeanne Alford

Communications and Media Coach

An experienced speaker, trainer, writer and PR expert, Jeanne Alford spent her career honing her expertise in communications. She has directed national and international public affairs and public relations programs for several brands including Dolby, Philips Electronics and Visa. She has also worked with leaders at some of the most innovative start-ups in Silicon Valley. No matter what position she held, her focus remains on telling a compelling branding story.

Jeanne's communications and PR campaigns have changed media perceptions, garnered national and international awareness for issues and helped to strongly position executives as industry leaders

Today, Jeanne serves as the executive director for the Sudden Cardiac Arrest Association and host of the podcast, Cardiac Conversations (www.cardiacconversations.org). She continues to work with individuals and small businesses to tell their most captivating stories—in the media, with customers and among their colleagues. Her focus is on developing communications strategies and coaching business leaders to elevate and refine their message.

Jeanne, a best-selling co-author and writer, published several business articles, white papers and marketing campaigns. Her materials have appeared in daily newspapers, national business publications and on several online sites. She most recently authored "3 Magic Questions to Instantly Improve Your Communications," which is available to download at BeClear101.com.

She has contributed to *Expert and Influencer Series: Leadership Edition, Bloom Where You Are Planted and Shine Step Forward and Shine* and the soon to be published, *Break Free to Stand in Your Power.*

Email: jeanne@alfordcommunications.com
Phone: 415-971-3344
Websites: alfordcommunications.com, beclear101.com
Facebook: https://www.facebook.com/BeClear101
LinkedIn: https://www.linkedin.com/in/jeannealford

Twitter: @jealford
Instagram: alfordj2000

SECTION 2:

Stand in Your Power

THE GRACE OF UNEXPECTED GIFTS
BY MARY E. KNIPPEL

"Something's wrong," I heard my son-in-law breathlessly say. "You have to come now!" It was six a.m. on April 4 and I was calmly getting ready to start my morning writing ritual when the phone interrupted me. I'm shaking now and barely avoided spilling my teacup at the Air B&B I'd rented to be close while my daughter was on maternity leave.

So began another opportunity to embrace the grace of unexpected gifts.

I'm not talking about something arriving from Amazon or a cute nick knack. I'm talking about those unexpected gifts that come wrapped in fear and frustration tied up with compassion and grace. Gifts in the form of life changing experiences. Life as you know it changes in an instant.

Every single circumstance that has happened . . . to us, for us, by us . . . have led us to this moment right now. It has led you to picking up this particular volume and choosing this passage to stop and read. All of us who search for the answers to who we are and what is the purpose of this life we have been given each day. I write these words for you. I write them for me. I write for all of us.

Life delivers challenges on a daily basis. Anything from misplaced keys, being late for an important meeting, to forgetting to pick up milk . . . which do have an impact on your life. Although, at the time, you don't see the significance to the extent that major life events do . . . your husband loses his job and he finds a great new one but it's three states away from all your family and friends. Or you get a form letter in the mail telling you that you have an abnormal mammogram and you need to call the doctor immediately, and that's your first of two breast cancer diagnoses. Or you become a grandmother for the first time, the baby arrives three weeks early, and you're over the moon excited. Then, when the baby is eight-days-old, your daughter, an otherwise healthy 35-year-old young woman, has a stroke which leaves her paralyzed on her left side and unable to care for this beautiful baby.

All your life experiences have brought you to where you are right now. What is important to shine the light on here is how you receive those unexpected gifts, how you cope with them and, most importantly, what you do next. Those life-altering experiences provide the opportunity for you to step into owning your story. To shine as the Hero you are in your own story and show the world you are a phenomenal Hero and not just a supporting player in somebody else's story.

No matter what the situation, you have the power to take action. You are never powerless. Although, you may temporarily feel less powerful than you want.

They say that the major stressors in our lives are loss of a job, loss of a loved one, major move, catastrophic illness or divorce. Except for the divorce part, I've experienced all of these stressors at least twice. Well, I have to admit because I've been married since 1972, there have been many ups and downs in our relationship. Neither one of us is the same 21-year-old we were when we exchanged those vows. I am tremendously grateful that there have been a significant number of "better" days and wildly appreciative that we have weathered those "worse" days.

Our current situation has me delighting in my new role as a doting grandmother while navigating the reality that our vibrant, health conscious daughter who gave up all caffeine and watched for any hint of distress in utero, had a stroke when the baby was a week old. They live hundreds of miles away from us with no other family to help care for the infant or my daughter and son-in-law. Although surprised and dazed by the severity of the situation and with the full support of my husband, I picked up and moved to the area where they are living to be close at hand to help the new little family. My daughter and son-in-law (who is legally blind and has battled diabetes since he was 5) seemed bewildered that I would uproot my life just to be close to the baby.

It's not as simple as that. The real story is in the details. Since the day of the stroke, my daughter has been at death's door in the intensive care unit no less than four times. She has limited use of her left side. She can walk with the use of a cane as she essentially drags her left foot along. Her left arm hangs by her side and her hand is similarly lifeless. She suffers from debilitating seizures and takes numerous medications to manage her many symptoms.

It breaks my heart that my daughter is the mother of this beautiful angel and cannot cradle her in her arms to comfort her when she cries or feed her when she is hungry. The silver lining is that my daughter has never lost her ability to communicate verbally, nor any of her cognitive skills. She reads to her little girl whenever she can. She is involved in decisions about the baby's welfare and researches what kind of diapers to use, which organic foods to buy and what type of clothing she wants the baby to wear. **She is doing what she can to be the kind of mother she wants to be to her daughter.**

I am doing what I deem necessary to be the kind of mother and grandmother I want to be for my daughter and granddaughter.

It sounds simple. The real story is in the details. I want to be 15 minutes away rather than 15 hours away when they need me.

Maybe that was too drastic—but I ask you—**what would you do if you were faced with a dramatic situation? What if you were presented with an impossible decision?**

Yes, I temporarily put my life on hold to ensure a secure and solid foundation for my granddaughter, daughter and son-in-law. My desire for my daughter to have a healthy recovery path, provide a solid support system for my son-in-law and a thriving environment for my granddaughter is my only priority at this point in time.

Life is one blessed thing after another.

A breath, a choice, which direction to go, stay or leave.

Where do we have control?

Where don't we have control?

How do we live day-to-day with the choices we make?

Know that we matter.

Know that we are making a difference in this world by being our unique selves and living our lives with all the love, compassion and creativity we can cram into it. To follow our dreams and share our gifts and talents with the world.

While I struggle to find a balance in my commitment to being here for my loved ones and my commitment to self-care, I know that I am the only one who could make myself a priority. By speaking up for what I need and taking time for myself, everyone in my life benefits. Self-care doesn't have to be elaborate or time consuming, but it is critical that you do have to decide what feeds your body, mind and spirit and then go do them! Sometimes, it is sitting in the sunshine with a cup of tea, a massage, a manicure and a pedicure, or a long soak in the tub. Other times, it is going on a week-long trip to Paris with a girlfriend, or gathering with like-minded women at a conference out of town. **You decide what will nourish you and fill yourself up on a regular basis.**

When I was a little girl growing up on the farm in the Midwest, writing was not something anyone encouraged me to do. Writing wasn't practical, but my fast typing skills and spelling knowledge earned me a One-Year Secretarial certificate and a job at the corporate office of the area's major employer. **It's up to us to choose if lack of encouragement is cause for permanent dismissal or an opportunity to adjust our dreams so that we achieve them via a different path.**

My dream of being a writer hasn't changed. I may not have my own book on the best seller list, yet, but my words are out there having an impact through my blogs, articles and the talks I share with the world.

I'm here to talk about how life delivers unexpected gifts as road blocks on our path. Stop signs that give us pause and force us to halt in our tracks. Wake up calls that make us pay attention and take action. Regardless of what sounds the alarm, there is one strategy I've used to navigate life's challenges. Rest assured, it is not a tool to buy, a gadget to master, or a skill that requires expensive equipment. In fact, I'm sure it's something you've had experience with since you were a child. Have you guessed yet?

This wonderful coping strategy is writing in a journal. Writing in my journal has helped me in so many ways to uncover the dreams I'd been hiding from myself and to discover ways to live my dreams. Everything I have accomplished personally and professionally started in my journal. ***I invite you commit to writing for just five minutes a day and be amazed by what will come to the surface when you take dictation from your soul and receive your inner wisdom.***

While certain times of your life can give pause (a milestone birthday, a significant anniversary, the death of someone close to you, an accident or a catastrophic illness), it takes something really big in your life to have us take some sort of action and make changes. In my case, I thought I was pretty content leading the life I had always dreamed of having. My husband had a good job and provided a beautiful life for us. We had adopted a sweet baby girl and were a family. I had achieved my goal of earning a college degree and landed a part-time job as an editorial assistant for a monthly newspaper. I'd weathered some major life transitions and coped pretty will with uprooting our family twice.

With my first breast cancer diagnosis and surgery, I threw myself back into my normal routine as quickly as I could. I believe that I wanted to pretend that first diagnosis never happened.

Three years later, the second diagnosis in the same breast. I was forced to stop and pause. My physical world and my inner world demanded I pay attention. Has that ever happened to you? Was there ever a time where you ignored whispers to slow down, take a breath or linger a while? And the more you pushed through to try and "make it happen," you became upset and frustrated that what you wanted to have happen was not happening. The whisper turned into a howling that would not go away until you paid attention. That nagging feeling of something important will not be put off. And life as you know it changes in an instant.

Today, I am no longer content to be shy, quiet Mary who went along with whatever others decided. Where can you step out a little bit more, sharing more of you and your gifts? Mine was in writing, leadership roles, speaking and helping others. **You must decide what is right for you and take action.**

I am on a mission now to encourage everyone not to wait until they have a crisis to make changes. Life is too short to wait. You are too important and what you have to offer is too valuable; don't wait.

You can bring your dreams to life, and journaling is the path to get there by capturing it on paper.

The most valuable advice I can share with you is to pick up a pen and write (longhand) in a journal. It's the most incredible tool to be able to connect your heart with your head and literally see your thoughts on the page. Whether you ever want to share those words with the world, it is important that YOU gain the insights and wisdom of your inner knowing. Your journal is a refuge, resource and record of your life. It can help you focus, keep you grounded, and not only remind you where you've been; it is a vehicle to propel you forward.

Just the way some have a meditation practice or a yoga practice, **I encourage every woman to have a writing practice**. Spend time alone with your journal every day. Pick a time you can show up consistently and block out time on your calendar just for you and your journal. It doesn't have to be long; five to fifteen minutes will allow you to establish a writing practice. Choose a pretty notebook and a fast-writing pen. Always put the date and time at the top of the page. Describe your surroundings to ground yourself in time and space. Set the timer and go. Keep your pen moving until the timer goes off.

This is your chance to listen to what your heart wants to say to you. A chance to have a conversation with your soul.

Life is a blessing. Everything that has happened in your life has made you who you are today. I've been given an opportunity to have a very special relationship with my granddaughter and to not only tell my daughter how much she means to me, but to show her I'd be willing to do anything to help her achieve a happy, healthy life. That's my bigger story.

I believe writing in your journal can help you explore and go deeper into you discovering your bigger story.

Allow yourself the gift of at least 30 days to anchor the writing practice into your routine.

I've created a simple journal for you to download containing some of my favorite quotes for inspiration. Just go to https://yourwritingmentor.com/2016jgift/

Embracing the grace of unexpected gifts means you meet whatever Life brings you with an open mind and heart because you have the strength to cope with whatever it is, the guts to not back down from this challenge and incredible creativity to turn that unexpected gift from tragedy into triumph. ***It is no coincidence that the bonus of these unexpected gifts is you having the opportunity to get to know someone you have been longing to meet on a very intimate level . . . YourSelf.***

Embracing Unexpected Gifts

1. Everything has led to this moment.
2. Be willing to find the gift.
3. Listen to your soul and heart.
4. Practice self-care for you.
5. Choose who/how you want to be & do it.

Mary E. Knippel

As a child growing up in Middle America, Mary E. Knippel dreamt of making a difference in the world. Exactly how she'd do that wasn't clear to her or anyone else since she was a shy and quiet kid who pretty much melted into the background. Today she helps people who are blocked in writing to find the freedom to know they have the ability to write. Specifically, to transform those unexpected gifts of life experiences that come wrapped in frustration and fear from tragedy into triumph. A best-selling author, inspirational speaker, and the Writer Unleashed at YourWritingMentor.com, she makes a difference by being your Champion, Architect and Cheerleader, supporting you to unleash your story worth writing and to shine in your business . . . and your life. With a firm philosophy that *No one can tell your story but* YOU, Mary invites you to take pen in hand to deliver your story's unique message to the world. Using her 35 years as a journalist and the power of storytelling, she helps you gain clarity and confidence in your story and who needs to hear it. As a journal writer since the age of 11, Mary knows the enormous power and healing capabilities of the written word. A two-time breast cancer survivor, she used writing and other creative tools in her recovery and chronicles the results in her book, *The Secret Artist*, where she shares what she has learned to help you move from survive to thrive. Learn more about Mary at http://yourwritingmentor.com.

Mary@yourwritingmentor.com
650-440-5616
https://yourwritingmentor.com
Facebook: https://facebook.com/maryeknippel.author
https://facebook.com/maryeknippel
LinkedIn: https://www.linkedin.com/in/maryeknippel
Twitter: https://twitter.comMEKnippelAuthor
YouTube: https://www.youtube.com/user/maryeknippel
Instagram: https://www.instagram.com/maryeknipppel
Pinterest: https://www.pinterest.com/maryeknippel/

SUFFERIN' 'TIL SUFFRAGE
BY AERIOL ASCHER

The year was 1976 on any given Saturday. I was fully clad in a purple Danskin leotard and a make-shift red cape with a hairbrush grasped firmly in my microphone hand as I leapt off the family couch at grandma's house. Mom was taking another shift at work, which always seemed to be the case. I enthusiastically belted out one of my favorite songs "Sufferin' 'til Suffrage" from the Schoolhouse Rock cartoon featured on Saturday morning TV programming at the time:

"Now you have heard of Women's Rights,
And how we've tried to reach new heights.
If we're all created equal, That's us too!"
"Sufferin' Till Suffrage" Schoolhouse Rock

I was drenched in sheer girl power. Fully expressed, singing my heart song, channeling my inner super powers, nothing could stop me, yes THAT girl was on FIRE! And then, I remember that Grandma decided to use this as a teaching moment to tell me all about how her mother had marched to earn our equal rights and how important the Women's Suffrage Movement had been. OK. I just loved this song. I leaned in to hear my grandmother's story unfold. I was amazed by what she told me. Some people don't think women are as good as men, she told me. Some people do not think women should be considered equal to men. I was stunned. I did not know exactly how to process this.

The thought of being less than because I was a girl or denied something because I was a girl was such a foreign concept from my young and super self-expressed perspective it has always stuck with me. When I look back at this moment, I cannot help but marvel at how bizarre what my grandmother was telling me was from my perspective of empowered innocence. **Surely it was not true that there was a grown up world out there where girls were not allowed to speak? To vote? To go to school? Surely grandma must be mistaken. But she was not mistaken.**

"But you will prob-a-bly not recall
That it's not been too, too long at all,
Since we even had the right to
Cast a vote."
"*Sufferin' 'til Suffrage*" Schoolhouse Rock

The stacks of Ms. Magazines on the coffee table in front of our old 14" screen black and white TV console had informed me that we were all free to be you and me, whatever that meant. I remember quoting one of Ms. Magazine's feminist headlines for a cursive handwriting assignment around this time in my life. I carefully and proudly wrote in my newly acquired script with my pointy, sharp number two pencil: a woman's place is in the house, and senate. My third grade teacher gave an A on that assignment. She also told me I was very ambitious and idealistic. I think I had to look those words up in my hardbound Webster dictionary when I got home, but I was pretty sure that was good.

Fast forward, now decades later in my own life and in fact an entire century after my grandmother's mother had marched with the women's suffrage movement against the injustices of her country's laws in order to create a new law that women were equal to men and were able to vote. The opportunity to submit this chapter was presented to me, and I was intrigued and excited to participate in a book on Women's Empowerment. It seemed like a perfect fit, and yet when I sat down to write this chapter, I have to be perfectly honest, there was a moment that I got really sad that we even have the need to use the term women's empowerment. **Grandma**

was right. We still had a long way to go and long after her passing we still do. Why is it that we live in a world where women need so desperately to be empowered? The fact of the matter is, we do. The fact of the matter is that women make up half the population on the planet but are not represented in leadership as prominently as their male counterparts and still do not make equal wages in the work place.

"Oh, we were suffering until suffrage,
Not a woman here could vote, no matter what age,
Then the 19th Amendment struck down that restrictive rule."
"*Sufferin' 'til Suffrage*" Schoolhouse Rock

Now, don't get me wrong, I did not grow up to go into politics or even have much interest in it, but I have to say it is such an interesting and exciting time we live in. Our systems, politics and beliefs are in some sense breaking down and we are in need of great change. We are constantly being shown how we must evolve and adapt to bring into balance some very serious social and environmental issues that will effect generations to come. **Although at times it seems like we are on the brink of war and environmental destruction, there is a really fantastic opportunity for more women to step up, to speak up and to be seen in roles of leadership. Our voices and our presence have never been more needed in order to bring our world into balance.**

"And now we pull down on the lever,
Cast our ballots and we endeavor
To improve our country, state, county, town, and school."
"*Sufferin' 'til Suffrage*" Schoolhouse Rock

So what can we do to empower ourselves and our voices as women in our world landscape? How can we step up and be leaders at this time? What changes can we implement to improve our country, state, county, town and school, as my childhood song imprinted across my heart so many years ago?

<u>Know yourself and strive for a high level of self-awareness</u>. Know who you are and what you stand for. To accomplish this, you have to invest time in getting to know yourself and to develop a routine of something I call whole selfcare. I talk about this quite a lot in my work just as a way for us to tease apart the aspects of what we refer to as the self. By whole self-care I mean the physical, mental, emotional and spiritual aspects of our self as a whole. Feel into each of the areas of yourself and investigate how you are showing up in your world and how you feel about your life. By examining the self as whole, you will be able to determine what areas may have imbalances, which are caused by either excess or deficiency in any certain area. Where are you deficient? Where are we sufficient, and what do you excel at? Know yourself.

Listen to yourself. This goes hand in hand with the whole self-care concept we already covered. But it warrants its own discussion. Take the time to develop a deep connection and relationship with the self. Listen to your thought narratives, intuition and instincts. To do this you must be grounded into the planet, be centered in your own heart and connected to your own divine source energy. By taking time daily to establish a grounded connection with yourself and the divine, you begin to create a more authentic and rich experience.

It is only by listening to your own inner voice that you can access a true level of discernment between your thoughts and ideas and energies and those of others. It is here where you can start tapping into your own wisdom and your own truth. Once you have a sense of being connected to your own source energy, you can direct your energy in ways that support you, your loved ones and your greater community.

Care for yourself in ways that support the whole you. For example, someone may find it easy to care for their basic physical needs but not to connect emotionally to others. Or maybe someone leans towards being more analytical or logical rather than coming from their heart. By adding awareness to emotional self-care and incorporating it into daily practice, a more balanced self will be able to emerge. If you do not care for the physical needs of your body, you notice right away if you are not being supported. It takes a little more diligence to discover the nuances of how the energetic and emotional pieces shape and affect our lives. I will say that it is my observation as a healing practitioner that if someone cuts themselves off to their spiritual nature so that they cannot trust or access their own intuition or inner knowingness, they often suffer from anxiety or depression. Likewise, stuffing unprocessed emotions will always eventually show up in the physical body as some sort of condition of dis-ease.

Take Responsibility for your life circumstances whenever possible. If there is something that is holding you back or causing an imbalance in your life, be brave enough to witness what it is and course correct. Find the silver lining in challenges, or at least have faith that over time the wisdom of a situation will always be revealed.

Use your Voice. I could talk for days about using your voice and what that means to me. I am a vocalist and musician and well as a sound healing practitioner so I often speak of the benefits of vibration and tone and share practical vocal exercises for awakening the body using the voice. There are plenty of physical and emotional benefits to singing and the breath work that goes along with vocalizing on a regular basis. So I recommend cultivating the voice on many levels. But for the sake of this women's empowerment chapter, let me open the conversation on voice here: **your voice is how you present your divine self into the world.** Your intention, energy, thoughts, breath and words all combine and manifest themselves as your perfectly unique voice and vibration. This is the expression of who you are. So you see, your voice truly matters. It is how you communicate, it is how you connect with others, it is how you exist and, most importantly, it is how to create change in your world.

"Then Susan B. Anthony (Yeah!) and Julia Howe,
(Lucretia!) Lucretia Mott, (and others!) they showed us how;
They carried signs and marched in lines
Until at long last the law was passed."
"*Sufferin' 'til Suffrage*" Schoolhouse Rock

Take Action. What action steps can we take to support all this inner self care work to bring our empowered voices forward in the world? Here are a couple of things you can do to start to develop a daily self-care practice and a success vision plan. This list is by no means complete but just some of my ideas on how to direct your energies to be the most effective.

1. Take time daily to do some sort of meditation that includes conscious deep breathing.
2. Identify your mission and visualize yourself achieving your mission on a regular basis. Expect success.
3. Check in with yourself by journaling on a regular basis for gratitude, intention setting, vision crafting and daily reflection.

4. Embody self-certainty by knowing yourself and understanding your motivations. Remember, confidence is magnetic.
5. Develop excellent communication skills. Even if you have wonderful ideas or intentions, when they are not presented in a way that is effective your ideas won't be executed.
6. Invest in yourself. You are your most valuable asset. Always continue to educate yourself by committing to being a lifelong learner so you will always be growing.
8. Get published! In our age of media, it has never been easier to give your voice form by publishing a book, an article or even a blog post in order to share your wisdom / perspective.
9. Get out into the world and speak. People need to hear what you have to say and see what you stand for.
10. Empower others. Share your resources with those in need. Pave the way for the women of tomorrow. Pass it on. Teach what you have learned.
11. Learn to cultivate relationships. Consciously gather a like-minded community. Surround yourself with people you like and admire.
12. Lead.

I guess the real bottom line I am trying to convey is to figure out what you stand for, what you believe in, and then speak up for what you stand for and what you believe in. When you are connected and have the greatest good in mind, you just do your thing. **So go ahead. Use your voice. Know you count. Know you are enough. Know you matter. Express yourself. Most importantly, if and when your opportunity arises, take your turn. You were put here for this exact reason at this exact moment, this exact point in history. You are here on purpose.** You are a change maker. A bringer of peace. A speaker of truth. A shining light. Now, go and do your thing.

"And now we pull down on the lever Cast our ballots and we endeavor
To improve our country, state, county,
town, and school
Since 1920 . . .
Sisters, unite!
Vote on!"
"*Sufferin' 'til Suffrage*" Schoolhouse Rock

I just know that the women of past generations are standing behind all women at this time. If you listen closely, you will hear their voices cheering you on. **Take action. Rise up. Use your powerful voices to bring healing to our world. We are all counting on you.**

Aeriol Ascher, MsD.

Aeriol Ascher, MsD. Author, Speaker, Master Metaphysician, Empowerment Leader and Presence Coach has been in the field of self-care and personal development for 25+ years. Before closing the doors of her Holistic Healing Center, Reiki Angel Intuitive Arts, it was voted Best Day Spa in Silicon Valley by the San Jose Mercury News, and her signature service, the Reiki Angel Massage, was voted best massage four times.

Aeriol empowers her audiences and clients with tools that increase awareness, hone intuition and connect to their highest self so they can confidently show up, speak up and stand out in their personal and professional lives. She has a passion for facilitating group experiences that awaken self-awareness, inspire growth and empower audiences with lots of fun.

An advocate of self-expression and women in leadership, Aeriol loves to assist her clients to embody their most powerful presence and let their whole soul shine. Hailing from a Stage and Media Production background, Aeriol loves to write and she hosts a weekly podcast, **Healing Body, Mind and Soul**, in which she publishes empowering conversations with Master Practitioners, New Thought Leaders and Transformational Coaches worldwide to speak about a variety of whole self-care topics.

Aeriol is available for speaking engagements, group and individual trainings, coaching and private healing sessions, both in person or via video conferencing technology. Aeriol lives in San Jose, CA with her fur family consisting of three small dogs, Ziggy, Twinkie & Dali, and their wise old cat Aengus.

More about Aeriol: www.AskAeriol.com
Healing Practice: www.SomaSoundTherapy.com
VoiceAmerica.TV Show: www.HealingBodyMindandSoul.com
Social Links:
www.facebook.com/askaeriol
www.facebook.com/somasoundtherapy
www.instagram.com/askaeriol/
www.twitter.com/askaeriol
www.youtube.com/user/ReikiAngelMassage
www.linkedin.com/in/aeriolascher/

YOU CAN ALWAYS CHOOSE BLISS
BY MONEEKA SAWYER

"Decision is the spark that ignites action. Until a decision is made, nothing happens . . . . Decision is the courageous facing of issues, knowing that if they are not faced, problems will remain forever unanswered."
~ *Wilfred A. Peterson*

As I thought about what I wanted to share with you, I was inspired by a chapter from my book *Choose Bliss: The Power and Practice of Joy and Contentment*. That book is all about empowering us to choose the life our hearts deeply desire. In this chapter, I wanted to delve into the idea that even **though we can't control what happens to us, we can always control how we choose to respond.** Do we allow setbacks stop us? Or do we instead allow what we learn from them to propel us forward to our better life? I hope through this chapter you will be inspired to always choose bliss.

When David and I got married, we decided we were not going to have children. At that time, that choice really made sense for us. But as I got older, my maternal instincts kicked in, and I changed my mind. I needed to make a tough choice at that point. Should I bring it up and possibly lose my husband, or should I keep it inside and possibly regret it for the rest of my life? Sometimes we need to make really tough choices. I took a huge risk and decided to talk to David.

"But we agreed that we didn't want children," David said.

We were sitting on a bench in Paris waiting for the train to take us to Lyon.

"We also agreed that we would talk about it if I ever changed my mind," I replied.

We sat in silence for a while, not knowing how to move forward from there.

Thus began the first of many train station conversations about babies. At the time, we were living in Lyon, France, and David was always in a good mood when we were embarking on a new adventure. It seemed like the best time to engage him on the topic of starting a family.

So we had the conversation on train benches in Paris, Lyon, Carcassonne, Strasbourg, Nice, and many others. Eventually, David agreed. "All right," he said. "Let's try."

In Paris, we conceived. I was overjoyed!

I had no problem getting pregnant.

But then, just as I was completing my first trimester, I miscarried.

Although I had a history of miscarriages, this was the first time David and I were intentional about starting a family. I was devastated. David, I suspect, was a little relieved.

When we got back to the United States, I redoubled my efforts.

I tried everything to ensure that I would succeed. Traditional Western medicine. Fertility clinics. Hormone injections. Acupuncture. Energy work. Strict nutritional approaches.

It consumed our attention, our focus, our lives, and our resources. Fertility work is expensive.

One evening as we were having dinner at a restaurant, David said, "I don't think I can do this."

I'm not sure if David just assumed that I would never carry a baby to full term, or if he didn't count on my commitment being so intense and so costly. In any event, he was done.

I looked at him with compassion and conviction and replied, "You can't tell a woman she can't have children. You need to decide."

He did. And he left.

Our separation was short-lived. David returned after a couple of weeks.

"This is really stupid," he said. "I love you. I want to support you in this."

It was David's turn to choose his bliss, and he chose to connect his bliss to mine.

*****

The doctor smeared the cold gel on my abdomen and moved the wand over and back, over and back.

I lay there, looking up at the white ceiling and the fluorescent lights. I had been on three months of complete bed rest, so I was all too familiar with lying down.

I was feeling really good about this pregnancy. Everything was aligned. Everything felt right. I had given myself until I turned forty-two to have a child. That birthday was just a few months away. This was it!

The doctor removed the wand and readjusted the position of the monitor. She put the wand back on my stomach and moved it around again.

She had a strained, tight look on her face.

"Doctor?"

She removed the wand and looked at me.

"I think we lost the heartbeat."

"What?"

"There is no heartbeat. I'm so very sorry."

It didn't register. This was my fourteenth pregnancy. Each one had ended in a miscarriage at the end of the first trimester.

"Oh, that must be so hard for you to tell people," was all I could say.

The doctor left the room. I just sat there. I sat there on the end of the examination table in the sterile white room, shocked with my dead baby on the screen.

I started to cry. Then, I couldn't cry at all.

I walked out of the medical center, got into my car, and then it came. I sat there in the parking lot and sobbed.

In my experience, after a miscarriage, the baby would be released by my body the following week. It was always traumatic, but I knew what to expect.

A week passed, and then another. After three weeks, the doctor scheduled a DNC.

Weeks after the procedure, I was still in intense pain, both physical and emotional. I still felt my child inside of me, and then the physical pain of the doctor going in and yanking it out.

More time passed. I still couldn't sleep because I was in so much pain.

One night, I turned to David and said, "I just can't do this anymore. I have to find a way to be happy without a baby." As he held me that night, I cried deep, soulful, healing tears.

After my decision, the response from my family and friends was supportive but hard to take. I told my parents that we were going to stop trying, and they cried with me. They felt my sadness. They felt their own.

The conversations always turned to considering other options. Could you adopt? Could you get a surrogate?

I asked David, "If I really decided that I want to adopt, would you be all right with that?"

"Absolutely," he said.

Everyone knew how much I had tried to have a child. I was so maternal and invested.

But in the end, I decided that I was done.

"No," I would say. "No, no. I just lost fourteen children. I need to recover. I need to move on."

My well-meaning family and friends would say things like, "Are you sure?" and "Maybe you'll regret this."

In the end, although all these voices in my life were trying to support me, I had to stand up for myself and stop the conversation. It was time for some deep soul searching. It was time for some self-care.

The major turning point in my life came when I decided that no matter whether I had a child or not, I could and would choose bliss.

This allowed me to reconcile what I thought I wanted with what I had—and with what I may never have.

Six months after that last miscarriage, my dear friend Paula called me and invited me to lunch.

"I had a dream about you last night," she said.

"Oh?"

"Yes. In my dream, we had a baby together," Paula said.

"What? What do you mean?"

Paula looked at me intently. "Moneeka, if you still want to have a baby, I would love to be your surrogate."

I started to cry. What an amazing gift from one of my closest friends.

I told her, "No," and we cried together.

It was in that moment that I knew I had chosen bliss. As much as this loving offer to help could have brought a child into my life, I knew that I had made my decision. And my decision was not to have children.

When I knew that I had a viable option—a truly good option—to have my own biological child, and my heart still held to its resolve, I knew that I had made the right choice. It wasn't resignation. It was a positive stand, a decision to move forward for myself.

In that moment, I realized that we—you, I, everyone—get to make our choices and live with those choices. It is in the choosing where you will truly find your bliss.

I made another choice. I would not be "the woman who couldn't have children." That was a part of my history, my learning, but it wasn't my story. It didn't define me. The choice is mine who I want to be. I define me.

Obstacles in life happen. But remember that you get to choose how you define yourself. You get to choose how your life will be. And, no matter what, you can always *Choose Bliss*.

Tips for Finding Your Bliss

1. Remember, no matter what happens in life, you still have choice.
2. Discover what is important to you and choose that.
3. Listen to your heart and align your decisions to your heart's desires.
4. Choose carefully and purposefully how you define yourself.
5. Choose your Bliss!

Moneeka Sawyer

Moneeka Sawyer is the blissful millionaire. She reached her financial freedom by turning $10,000 to over $2,000,000 working only 5-10 hours per MONTH with very little stress. She hosts a highly rated radio show and has interviewed prestigious guests such as Leeza Gibbons, Dr. Joe Vitale, and Hal Elrod. She has been featured on stages with Suzanne Sommers, Martha Stewart, and Ice T and Coco at places like the Nasdaq Marketplace, Harvard, and Carnegie Hall, and on TV on NBC, CBS, ABC, and Fox, reaching over 150 million people.

Through her experience, Moneeka has created a system to make building wealth blissful. What do I mean by blissful? Bliss is a deep sense of joy and contentment. It's emotional resilience and emotional mastery.

What does bliss have to do with real estate? Warren Buffet says, "If you can't control your emotions, you can't control your money."

So, you can see that emotional mastery, or living in your bliss, is key to creating wealth through real estate long-term. If you run your real estate business blissfully, instead of it stressing you out, and burning you out, it adds to the joy (and success) in your life.

This has been Moneeka's path, and now she's on a mission to empower as many women as she can to build their own wealth blissfully. This will give them the freedom to do the things in life they really want to do and create the life their hearts most deeply desire.

social media:
https://www.facebook.com/MoneekaSawyer
https://twitter.com/moneekasawyer
Blissfulinvestor.com
Check out my weekly show at http://realestateinvestingforwomen-podcast.com/
Email Address: Moneeka@coreblisslife.com
Website: Blissfulinvestor.com
Facebook page(s) : https://www.facebook.com/MoneekaSawyer, https://www.facebook.com/BlissfulRealEstateInvestor/, https://www.facebook.com/groups/blissfulinvestor/
LinkedIn Page: Blissfulinvestor.com/LinkedIn

Twitter handle: @moneekasawyer
YouTube Channel: Blissfulinvestor.com/YouTube
Other Social Media Channels: Instagram @MoneekaSawyer

THE ACT OF GIVING PERMISSION
BY DR. NANCY TARR HART

"No one can make you feel inferior without your consent."
Eleanor Roosevelt

Consent is the act of giving one's permission; it is an act we often take for granted in our lives. But, giving permission that allows another to make you feel inferior? This is an act of giving that, more often than not, is neither expected nor purposeful, although admittedly there are some instances where we can actually anticipate that an individual will attempt to attack our self-worth. And, there are instances where they are successful because we have given them the permission they need to accomplish their mission. In other words, we can expect it in regard to some of the people we are surrounded with on our life's journey.

To complicate matters, we know that advertising and public imaging are powerful tools in our society—tools that can transform even the most confident of individuals into spirals of self-doubt, insecurity, and a general sense of being unworthy. Ads for travel, entertainment, clothing, and more tell us to give ourselves permission to enjoy exotic scenery—to "get away from it all," while auto and clothing ads often remind us that we are deserving of that new luxury car, the latest piece of portable technology, or the expensive designer wares that decorate the covers of magazines and storefront windows. Often, the implication is that we have either not been treating ourselves as well as we should have been, or that we generally don't deserve to be treated well as we're offered this one-time chance to cash in on prizes generally reserved for those who are more deserving—or superior—to us. Body images are attacked as societal norms are crafted to measure the acceptability of one's size, shape, or weight. Women's capabilities and qualifications for assuming positions of power traditionally held by men in this country are questioned and, in some cases, threatened through the use of gendered language or the simple act of not even considering possibilities. When was the last time a woman in political office, the space program, or in charge of a major company was referred to simply as a politician, astronaut, or CEO? We qualify women of power, referring to them as a woman politician or a female astronaut or CEO—another subtle but not so gentle reminder that, just perhaps, we are not as smart, not as strong or brave, not as worthy or deserving of being successful, being attractive, or being powerful as those more perfect folks around us.

Still, at first glance, it seems like consenting to feel inferior would be an easy choice to refuse—after all, there are plenty of others around who would gladly offer assistance in tearing down one's self-esteem and feelings of worthiness. However, after years of challenges surrounding this issue, I have come to the conclusion that it is difficult (if not impossible) to give consent to another and allow one's self to feel inferior if we haven't already beat others to the punch. In other words, we are active participants in this game of "give and take." And while it's highly unlikely that many of us consciously or intentionally think about turning the "attack" inward onto our own selves, it is this act of permission giving that is, more often than not, neither expected nor purposeful.

We end up not only controlling our choice of consenting to hand over our power to others, but in a sense, we lay the groundwork and set up the foundations to allow it to happen. We fall victim to our own devices and, as a result, open ourselves up to be manipulated, used, and (sometimes) abused by others.

But we cannot blame feelings of inadequacy or being inferior solely on external societal factors. We are just as guilty (and just as capable) of pulling the rug out from under our own feet—probably more often than we even realize. Think about it for a minute. When was the last time you passed up attending an event because you felt you didn't look your best? Did you skip a school reunion because someone would be in attendance that you hadn't seen for a while and you would have to explain that your career hadn't taken off in the same way in which theirs had? Or, maybe you didn't throw your name into the ring for that in-house promotion or submit your resume or express interest in a fabulous new job possibility due to the fear that you would probably be turned down because you weren't able to fulfill the requirements? Maybe you simply didn't introduce yourself to a person who caught your attention at an event because you felt that they probably wouldn't be interested in someone like you. These are all examples of giving consent—yes, to our own selves—to allow ourselves to feel inferior.

There are other instances that are far more insidious and so innocuous that we don't even realize what it is we're doing. To be sure, this can be very tricky ground to negotiate, and oftentimes we don't even realize we are giving ourselves permission to feel inferior. There is one instance from my own journey that begs to be shared because it exemplifies how unconscious our permission-giving is at times.

While time has blurred the edges and details of the memory—I cannot remember exactly what it was I was fussing at myself about—the most important parts of the story ring as true and clear as they did 30+ years ago. One of my work situations placed me within a cubicle-like office set-up; walls that did not reach the ceiling separated the administrative staff but did little to absorb the conversations and sounds of a busy office. I was at my desk and obviously had either made a mistake in a document I had prepared, or had done something that was wrong, inefficient, or both. As I realized this lack of accuracy, I reacted by saying out loud: "Nancy, you're an idiot!"

On the heels of my self-admonishment, I heard the voice of one of my officemates say, "Please don't talk that way about my friend, Nancy." It was a simple statement that not only stopped me in my tracks, but hit me at the core of my being. **She was saying what I often had trouble acknowledging, much less saying: not only was I *not* an idiot—I *was enough*. And, oftentimes, especially *when I stepped fully into my power*, I *was more than enough*. In other words, I was a mighty woman whose power was visible, palpable, and innate.**

But, over the years, there were times I put myself into a position of handing my power over to others who were more than happy to bring me to a place of being "lesser than" the powerful being I was intended to be—the truth of my existence. There were also times that I placed my power on a back shelf and out of my own reach because I allowed myself—gave permission to myself—to doubt my abilities and my inherent worth.

We are still left to ponder what it is that so often causes innately and otherwise powerful beings to so easily give permission and so often turn our permission-giving inward. Self-doubt (seeded by a multitude of factors that often begin in childhood) is a big one and probably sits near (if not at) the top of the list. So does comparing one's self with others. Why do we do this? We are, each of us, so totally unique and special, and we should be celebrating those gifts. Instead, we often use that uniqueness to our disadvantage when we compare ourselves and attempt to compete on a totally level playing field where everyone looks, acts, and thinks the same way. It just doesn't (and shouldn't) work that way. Unfortunately, in this reality, oftentimes it does.

My life's journey has been peppered with instances where I either consciously or unconsciously failed to realize my own worth, which manifested as not speaking up when I had something to offer at the table, by entering into unhealthy relationships, by not realizing my own potential in the work world, intellectually, or spiritually, by being self-effacing, and by not claiming or stepping into my own power. Whether it was dipping a toe into it or stepping into it to fully embrace it—claiming my own power was a real challenge *until* I stopped giving myself permission to feel inferior.

That is not to say there haven't continued to be times I have teetered on the precipice of self-doubt and inferiority. BUT, I have not taken the bait, put my power aside, or handed it over to another while stepping into the void and illusion of self-doubt and inferiority. Rather, it is those times that I find myself reasserting my strength and my resolve to be the wholly powerful woman who, for years, had parts of herself hidden behind the veils of uncertainty, self-doubt, and feelings of inadequacy held in place by a sense of unworthiness surrounding many areas of my life.

In looking back at what some would perceive to be my missteps, it becomes clear that there were learnings involved—learnings that sometimes needed repeating because I hadn't completely "gotten" the intended lesson. And, the lesson to be learned was so simplistic that it is almost embarrassing to admit to not "getting it." **It also is a lesson that *many* of us need to learn. It is a self-truth that we need to realize and hold near and dear to our hearts and souls: we are here to step into our full power—our full personhood—our fullness of being.** When we walk, talk, hear, and love through the universal truth that lives in our hearts, we realize that our power does not lie outside of ourselves. Our power is not something to seek, to access through others or other things (books, beliefs, etc.), or to compare to those around us. *Our power lies within us*; and, it is up to each one of us to admit to ourselves that no one is as uniquely qualified to be our own selves than we are. ***You are the answer, the lesson, the power.***

Although I am a firm believer in the fact that all happens at exactly the time that it should happen, I will confess to wishing I had learned the lesson a tad earlier than I did. Still, I will also admit that had someone shared the above wisdom with me earlier it's most likely I wouldn't have paid much attention. So, ultimately, I believe the timing was perfect for me to (finally) "get it" and step fully into my power. Doing so shifted my entire life journey's focus, putting me firmly on the path to my intended destiny and fulfillment of my purpose, and changing my life.

Now is the time for permission giving—giving one's self permission to move forward on your journey in love, compassion, strength, and yes, power—*your* power—the power that is uniquely yours to express. The act of giving permission to yourself to acknowledge, realize, and express that power is the choice you are here to make and to live. **When you have done so and fully accepted the beauty and worth of *you*, the words of Eleanor Roosevelt will never apply to you again. Trust in yourself. Trust in your gifts. Trust in your power—and soar!**

Nancy Tarr Hart, PhD

Nancy Tarr Hart, PhD has a wide and varied history of personal and professional experience with a career that encompasses working 40+ years in the worlds of business, education, and theatre. An intuitive and mystic, the understanding of her spiritual gifts fully ignited in 1995 and, in 1999 she was guided by Spirit/Sophia to begin an academic journey that began with working to attain an undergraduate degree. The journey culminated in a PhD in Religious Studies with a concentration in systematic theology, feminist theory, the Divine Feminine, and Marian Studies from the University of Wales Trinity Saint David in Lampeter, Wales. The author of the two-volume series entitled, *Beyond the Veil Volumes 1 and 2: Unmasking the Feminine* and *Unraveling the Mystery of Mary*, Dr. Tarr Hart is also a contributing author to *Empowering YOU, Transforming Lives* (compiled by Rebecca Hall Gruyter) and *Gateway to an Enlightened World: Collective Life Lessons to Support Planetary Transformation* (compiled by Dr. Ruth Anderson). Currently Chair & Assistant Professor, Department of Philosophy at the Notre Dame of Maryland University, she is an ardent fiber artist who enjoys traveling, reading, writing, gardening, and sharing her home with her cats, Kali and Bastet.

Contact Information:
Email: tarrheart@gmail.com
Website: www.walkinginwisdom.life
Facebook: https://www.facebook.com/nancy.t.hart.9
https://www.facebook.com/wisdom's.daughters.community.circles

WOMEN'S LEADERSHIP THROUGH TIME
BY AZUCENA PACHECO

Across time, women were taught to follow the orders of men. However, in every woman across generations there has been a desire to be different, and in today's times women have been gaining more ground in terms of leadership because nowadays women don't want to settle for less than what they are worth.

A female leader must have direction; that is why she looks up at God for compromise and direction, looks down on indecision, and side-eyes her old way of thinking and her lack of vision.

Men, according to our primarily patriarchal history, were positioned on this earth with the right to institute rules and norms. Humanity has seen the rise and fall of powerful monarchs, politicians, military tacticians and men of wealth and power. Unfortunately, with time, men have become indecisive, indifferent, with subpar morals, and unsure of themselves despite the position given to them.

In a perfect utopia the hierarchy of power would be followed as it was intended, with leaders at the top remaining uncorrupt and with the morals and credibility to effectively lead people. But we do not live in a perfect utopia; we live in the real world, and in the real world there is a high chance that our elected leaders and officials are not corruption-proof and more than likely there will always be a couple of people that do not want to follow their leaders just to be controversial or because they do not agree with who has been placed in power. People don't easily want to follow someone just because they are in a position of leadership. It doesn't matter whether the leader is a male or a female; what matters is presence, credibility and the ability to reach their community and inspire them.

Men and women act very differently when it comes to leadership. There are some very real differences in the way that they address people, conflict and just lead overall.

If we make a simple comparison, we see that:

Men:
- Are commanding at work
- Depend on his authority
- Inspire fear
- Think about the "me"
- Take care of the situation
- Are based on title
- Titles are won through being named

Women:
- Lead people, don't boss them around
- Depend on her kindness and charisma
- Inspire enthusiasm
- Think about the "we"
- Take care of the aftermath
- Are based on talent
- Titles are won through ability and perseverance

Men are more logical. They expect things to be done their way, exactly how they want them, when they want them. Meanwhile, women are gentler and want peaceful resolution when it comes to getting things done.

It is here that we find out that a great leadership must have these ingredients:

- People follow them because they want to
- They work without being forced
- They don't care how much knowledge they have because they care more about the people
- It begins with the heart and not the mind

- Works though inter-relationships
- Loves the people
- Gifts time and energy
- Can see other people's points of view
- Treats difficult people with wisdom

This is what makes a person a productive leader, because they follow him or her because of the results they see, and he or she meets their proposed goals.

This is a very similar context to Aristotle's rhetorical triangle: ethos, pathos, and logos. ++

- Ethos: Credibility – a leader must be trustworthy, they must be known.
- Pathos: Emotions and values – a leader must be willing to communicate openly with their audience and be in sync with their emotions, values and ideas.
- Logos: Message – a leader must have convictions! They must inspire trust trough their logic and their reasoning. They must be willing to be analyzed and evaluated.
 (WSJ/PathosEthosLogos.com)

There's something wonderful that happens with a female leader: she has influence.

Communication + Trust + Being known = Influence

Let's quickly define what influence is. Influence is the capacity to have an effect on the character, development, or behavior of someone or something, or the effect itself. Having influence on someone can inspire them to be not only followers, but to be active participants in what their leader is interested in and inspires a certain level of reciprocity.

There are certain factors and requirements that make a leader:

THREE UNIVERSAL FACTORS THAT MAKE A LEADER:

1. Satisfies needs
2. Fixes problems
3. Gives meaning

TWO REQUIEREMENTS

1. Have herself as a follower
2. Be willing to change

AKA: Has Influence! A leader must have influence on those who follow them! They must be a rock for whoever follows them; they must give a certain level of comfort and must be able to come through on their promises. A leader must also follow their ideals. They must do as they say. And most importantly, a leader must be flexible and willing to admit when they're wrong: they must be willing to change.

Men and women's leadership styles vary. Women, as stated previously, tend to be great influencers because they're great at gaining the trust of people, they're willing to lend an ear and help those who reach out for help. This might have something to do with the use of the brain's hemispheres.

USE OF THE BRAIN'S HEMISPHERES

LEFT:	RIGHT:
Logic, reason, vision	Emotions, intuition, creativity, ability to see colors

FUNCTIONS OF THE BRAIN'S HEMISPHERES

When the left hemisphere is more predominant, people:
- Are more systematic
- Are more logical
- Are more objective
- Are more aware of differences
- Are more structured
- Prefer certainty
- Are more analytical
- Are more focused on language
- Prefer to talk and write
- Control their feelings

When the right hemisphere is more predominant, people:
- Are more reckless
- Are more intuitive
- Are more subjective
- Are more aware of similarities
- Are more spontaneous
- Prefer flexibility
- Are more synthetic
- Are more focused on image
- Prefer to draw or act
- Freely express their feelings

Male leaders tend to be more logical. They want to resolve issues quickly and keep moving forward.

Women, on the other hand, take their time when it comes to conflict resolution and tend to be more willing to take more chances. There we can see that the women tend to be more right-hemisphere leaning.

WOMEN'S ROLE IN LEADERSHIP

Men who value and recognize that women are good allies and treat them as such are winners. Wise men value a woman's virtue and they listen to her advice. Such men are truly blessed.

This world produces conformity. God, on the other hand, produces individuality. God is not set on who His leaders will be. He does not have a mold set in place in which His leaders are forged. The last thing He wants is a carbon copy of followers. The Lord wants us to be unique individuals; he wants us to think differently, look different and have our own purpose.

Let's look at an example of this. Queen Esther was a woman who wretched from her people, was set to be queen because of her beauty. But Esther wasn't just beautiful, Esther was wise. Esther was respectful of her king, she was humble before her king, she gained the trust of her king and she was charming before her king. Esther wasn't just an influence on her king, Esther was a bona fide leader!

Another great example is Joan of Arc. Joan was a woman who was an influence on King Charles VII. Her victory with the Siege of Orleans was a morale booster for the French people. She gave them something to trust in and was a huge part on the French's victory. Joan was passionate, she was known, and she communicated her message: she was a leader with influence!

Women can absolutely be leaders. Women have been leaders throughout history; now it's just easier. Women have all the tools to be great leaders. It is just a matter of utilizing those tools and rising up to the challenge. A female leader must be a leader that has influence, and to have this influence she must keep in mind pathos, logos and ethos. She must be trusted, there must be a healthy channel of communication with her followers and she must be known—she must have credibility. While women have played more passive roles in our past, there have been some great leaders—female leaders—that have risen to prominence. As part of humanity, there is a certain level of responsibility as well. We must not be passive anymore; we must rise up and take charge. Let's set an example for sons and daughters. A leader has convictions! Tell your son or daughter who they can be, and they will have a goal! It is with this lofty goal in mind that we will raise great leaders with influence and with the ability to lead in whatever field they so choose.

++ The Wall Street Journal. PathosEthosLogos.com

Azucena Pacheco

Azucena Pacheco is a speaker and a PREPARE & ENRICH facilitator. She and her husband, Pastor Nicolas Pacheco, are church planters in the San Francisco Bay Area and founders of "Destruyendo Barreras," a marriage restoration ministry. Currently, both are serving at Iglesia Bautista Dulce Refugio in Oakland, CA. Azucena has a Christian Ministries Diploma from Gateway Seminary, formerly known as Golden Gate Baptist Theological Seminary.

azu.s.pacheco@gmail.com

SECTION 3:

Own Your Power and Shine!

YOUR INTERNAL AUTHENTIC VOICE IS YOUR COMPASS

BY ELLE BALLARD

Life gives us important directions and lessons at each new intersection of our lives and it is our responsibility to take them as such. If we listen to our internal voice and learn from our life lessons, we are able to move forward more intentionally and positively. I am sharing my lessons with you here and the way my internal authentic voice guides me in hope that they inspire, encourage and empower you.

I was born and grew up in Kazakhstan; right now it's a separate country, but at the time when I was born it was part of U.S.S.R., a communist country. I got married early to a person I loved so much. I was only 21 when we got married and I had my first child at 22. We had amazing feelings for each other, we would fall asleep and wake up hugging; we wanted to be together 24 hours daily. We frequently went to business meetings together and other gatherings.

I grew up in Kazakhstan, where cultural norms and beliefs are quite different from the western world standards. One of the local beliefs and traditions is that the youngest son or the only son has to live with his parents and bring his wife to the household. It does not matter whether parents are young or old at a time, it is a tradition and breaking it is considered a big shame.

I was brought up with different beliefs. I never had any idea about these kind of traditions, and since I loved my husband I decided to accept them and be a good respectful wife to my husband. I started learning the language as well and respected and followed all traditions at the expense of my own wishes and desires. I realized this was harder than expected and moreover, I realized I am losing who it is that I am, my own voice, my authentic self. We were together for three years and we have an amazing child together, but after three years I got really tired of limiting myself, forgetting myself and my desires and goals, losing my identity and my voice.

I left my husband and his family as I wanted to build a better life for me and my daughter. This was the first breakthrough of my life! I stayed with my grandmother with about four other people in a two-bedroom apartment with me and my daughter. No matter how uncomfortable it was and tiny, I felt such an amazing burst of freedom and happiness that I decided to continue to press on with my decision.

It was not easy. In a matter of days I found myself to be a single parent for my daughter with no help from outside except my own family. My ex-husband was too preoccupied with my decision to leave him and blamed me in everything, and even though had the means to provide for his daughter at a time, he decided not to. I am absolutely grateful for that experience as it became one of the main breakthroughs of my life and matured me at 25.

As I was a stay at home mom for three years and spoke only Russian, I had to re-learn my English from the beginning to be able to work as an interpreter/translator. This was the time when I had to start from the very beginning. **Lesson - Be flexible with situations, life and people. Be ready to adjust your course when needed. TRUST yourself and KNOW you can do it!**

After several years, I built a great career for myself in my city, was recognized professionally and bought a beautiful apartment for me and my daughter. I met my current husband in my office. He is an American who had been living in Russia for ten years and spoke beautiful and fluent

Russian, and in 2002 we moved to the U.S. Moving to the U.S. was one of the most important decisions of my life! Living in a completely new environment with a family and adjusting to a new environment is also one of the amazing lessons of my life.

While I was waiting for my U.S. visa to get approved in Moscow, Russia, I went to a modeling contest for fun and was offered to participate in two projects: one of them taking part in the well-known local magazine for a fall collection and another one to play a role in the movie. I really wanted to participate in those projects and knew how much fun I would have and the potential implications for my new exciting career! But I also knew what my priorities are, which were to reunite with my amazing husband, for my daughter to start school in a new country and help her adjust to a new environment. I made a decision to say 'No' to those offers, and once my visa was ready, I moved to Phoenix, AZ. **Lesson - We always know what to do in life intuitively; we just need to learn how to identify that voice and listen to it.**

Getting settled in the U.S., finding my passions took some time, and this was the second time when I had to start all over. It definitely took me a few years to get used to a new world, help my daughter settle here and learn the culture and language as I learnt British English before and not American English.

I recognized my ambitions and my drive, and I always knew I wanted to be in business for myself and that this country offers amazing opportunities for entrepreneurs. I did not know what the business would be or how it would look or where to start, so I decided to upgrade my degree, and after several GMAT and TOEFLE tests, I entered an MBA program and finished it in two years with Marketing concentration. I remember we had a round table with my MBA graduates to discuss what each of us really wanted, and I shared with a group how I wanted to be in business for myself. Everyone said they felt how my energy elevated when I talked about my passion and that I should pursue it. Instead, I decided to look for a job and spent the next seven years in a corporate environment working for software companies in a marketing capacity. I succeeded again. I had a great career, learnt a lot about marketing, achieved my goals and great income but was not fulfilled; I still dreamt about having a business and being an entrepreneur. I started a business on the side and got really passionate and excited about it but could not leave my job yet as my daughter was heading for college and I knew we will need to keep both of our incomes. But in 2014, my company was sold out and I lost my job. This is the third time when I had to start from the very beginning because this time I was moving from employee to entrepreneur.

My lessons and experiences shaped me and who it is that I am, my authenticity and my purpose. My passion of supporting and positively impacting women worldwide has been in me for a long time. My background of coming from a Muslim world and country, being a multicultural lady and my life experiences only strengthened this passion of supporting other women like me, independently if she is native born or a newcomer.

I found that women, whether native U.S.-born or immigrants, stay complacent and comfortable in their lives. Native-born ladies tend to underestimate how many opportunities we have in this beautiful country. If she is an immigrant, she sometimes stays in her comfortable native-speaking circles without realizing how much more she can become if she only let herself.

We as women can do so much.

We can take care of family AND our passions if we want to. We do not have to limit ourselves. My two daughters are future women; they are my main WHY I do what I do. I believe every woman can have it all IF she is willing to pay the price and IF she is willing to achieve bigger things. This has become my main reason and focus for giving back to the ladies like I am who might be going through the same experiences in their lives, for creating an authentic community for multicultural ladies.

With my vision in mind and my heart desire and my passion, I went ahead and launched my dream community, Women of the World Network, where we unite multicultural ladies from all backgrounds and ethnicities to grow, support and encourage each other while maintaining our strengths and authenticities. We officially launched in 2019. Right now we have ten chapters and growing! I have another business today that I am passionate about as well, and these two projects definitely keep me busy.

I always knew I wanted to become an entrepreneur but kept postponing it until it hit me that I need to make it HAPPEN even if I do not see the full picture yet. **Lesson - Always consult with your heart and your internal voice (it always guides you), then make a decision to start and**

take small steps to move forward towards your goals even if you are not seeing the full picture yet.

I could not finish this chapter and not write about how important it is to take care of YOU! Have you thought about what you are surrounded by? I mean everything that surrounds you in your life: people, thoughts, diet, sleep, rest. **It is so important to take care of YOU!** It is so important to take care of your health, eat well, rest, have enough sleep and periodically disconnect yourself from the day to day environment.

Your thoughts can be as toxic as people you surround yourself with. I just finished a twelve-day cleanse, and ballroom dancing is my favorite workout! Resting and taking care of you will give you strength, enhance your health and help you not only be able to give back more but also stay creative and energetic in your life. Pick that which allows you to rest and unwind. It is different for everybody. I discovered how important it is to surround myself with the right people who already think, have the life I want, live how I want, and at the same time NOT listen to people who have the life or wallet that I do not want. I learned to "love some people from the distance" to allow more time and energy for the people that I can learn from. At the same time, be flexible with people and situations and understand where they come from.

Lesson - On your journey do not forget to take care of your outer and inner world—people, your thoughts, your diet. Make sure to have a proper rest, engage in an activity that excites you and surround yourself with the right people and be intentional about the time you spend with people. You might need to spend three hours with some people, and with some others three minutes might be enough.

In conclusion, no matter what is happening around you, keep your vision and belief in check, listen to your inner voice and intuition, keep the right energy and vibration, take care of you, be ready to be flexible when you need to adjust your path and be ready to unlearn when needed! Give yourself permission to DREAM big, WIN big and GROW big. YOU deserve it!

Elle Ballard

Elle Ballard was born in Kazakhstan and has been living in the U.S. since 2002. She had a great career in Kazakhstan and a side business, and that is when her passion for entrepreneurship was born. When Elle came to the U.S., she had to start everything from scratch while supporting her family at the same time, but she always knew she wanted to be in business for herself.

Elle completed her MBA in Marketing and built a successful marketing career working for software companies in Houston, TX. While in the corporate world, Elle joined a Toastmaster speaking program and achieved a status of DTM (Distinguished Toastmaster).

She left the corporate world to pursue her true passion of impacting and helping people realize their true potential. Elle also completed the John Maxwell certification program and became a certified John Maxwell Speaker, Trainer and Coach.

Elle is a professional network marketer, certified John Maxwell speaker, mother and a founder of Women of the World Network. She is passionate about influencing and positively impacting others, and she is able to do that in both of her projects today. Despite all the challenges she faced, she always wanted to maintain her authenticity and who she is. This is a core reason for creating the Women of the World Network.

Email Address: elle@elleballard.com
Phone number: 832-202-3355
Website: www.elleballard.com
Website: www.womenoftheworldnetwork
Facebook: https://www.facebook.com/theelleballard/
LinkedIn: https://www.linkedin.com/in/elviraballard
Instagram: https://www.instagram.com/theelleballard/

TRUST YOURSELF TO MANAGE YOUR MONEY
BY DIANA MIRET

You are not fully empowered until you empower yourself over your money.

Some of us are forced to jump off the cliff of financial empowerment—ready or not.

On a sunny day in a glass high-rise downtown, our marriage of 22 years was picked apart, separated into piles of "she gets this, he gets that", terms and conditions, obligations, settlements, and animosity. Our lawyers gleefully picked apart the cadaver of our marriage as their $345 an hour rate climbed into the five figures. It was painful and embarrassing. Our private lives turned into fodder for discussion between two lawyers who didn't know us and really didn't care. The most painful part was looking at my soon to be ex-husband seething with rage and anger, glaring at me from across the table. Men learn early how to become warriors. The schools teach them how to be on a team and "fight" for victory. Some parents buy little boys toy weapons and they play soldier happily amongst the living room pillows. Most learn how to defend themselves in the schoolyard and in the boardroom. Movies and books are filled with scenes of men taking on corporate giants and bullies fighting for their territory. My soon-to-be ex-husband was a warrior and had experience in digging a trench and fighting. I, on the other hand, was completely out-gunned and out-manned. Pun intended. I had hired the expensive lawyer because I needed to level the playing field. I knew I was way out of my league. I was not a victim—not by any definition. I had chosen this path for private reasons, so I had to "buck up" and "be strong". Be empowered—even though I did not feel empowered. I, too, was a veteran of many boardrooms as part of my career and I knew one thing: whatever you do, don't cry. Don't show weakness. Be strong. Hold the line. Stare the person across the table down with a grim face. I doubt I fooled anyone that day.

After the meeting, I dissolved into tears in the washroom. My knees shook, as I threw up my breakfast from the anxiety. **Alone and wiping cold sweat from my face, I looked in the mirror and said aloud, "You better figure out what to do next because now you have to look after yourself."**

I went home on the train with my sunglasses on because I didn't want to be seen crying on public transit. Once home, I climbed into bed and did not get up for three days. I ate soup out of a can and cried. It was a painful time. I had a mixture of relief, regret, grief, guilt and anxiety. But that is not the subject matter of this chapter.

It took three days to get the strength together to put on my big girl panties. I had to go to work and present the status of a very complicated, mega expensive, strategic project to the CEO of the company. I also had an appointment at noon with a local bank branch manager. Little did I know that those two appointments were about to completely unravel me.

A stable marriage is one of the best paths to building and maintaining wealth, according to Forbes Magazine. Divorce, on the other hand, is expensive. Possessions, money, financial assets and debt acquired during (and sometimes before) marriage are divided between former spouses. In fact, divorcing individuals need a more than 30% increase in income, on average, to maintain the same standard of living they had prior to their divorce.(1)

Divorce is one of the most common ways that people, especially women and children, fall into financial difficulties. When this happens, they become dependent on government programs, services, and supports. Divorce and unwed childbearing cost U.S. taxpayers at least $112 billion each year.(2) These costs are just for public assistance programs (welfare), not the cost of the divorce itself (lawyer and court fees, counseling, mediation, etc.).

How does divorce financially affect women?

Women suffer more financially than men from divorce. The financial burden is greatest during the first year after divorce and varies depending on (1) how much money the woman contributed to the family income before divorce and (2) the ability and willingness of her former husband to make child support payments.

About one in five women fall into poverty as a result of divorce. The poverty level in 2019 for a household of four is an annual income of $25,750.(2)

The purpose of this chapter is not to delve into the complicated realm of the financial impact of divorce on women. That analysis is better left for sociologists to unpack. **My goal is to open women's eyes to the need to understand their financial standing, regardless of their marital status or age.**

In my experience coaching women business owners, **they are generally reluctant to look at financial aspects of their life until life MAKES them do it.** Like the vast majority of people who start exercising and eating well AFTER they receive the bad diagnosis from their doctor, women tend to not get involved with their money until they have no choice. They become, what I call, a Helpless Traveler.

In my experience as a traveler, I have met people who seem to get where they are going, know their way around and become the genius everyone wants to travel with. Somehow, they know where to find the best places to eat, they figure out the exchange rates, they know how much to leave as tip in a foreign currency and how to get to the hotel from the airport. Some people just "know". I have enjoyed travelling with folks like these. **The problem comes when we sit back and rely on these people and don't take an active role in the trip.** We become "helpless" travelers (so to speak) and ultimately go on a vacation or trip of someone else's design. You eat where they want to eat and do what they want to do and see the sites they want to see. I realize that this is a generalization and doesn't fully apply to every aspect of the trip, but I believe if you are honest with yourself, you will recognize this pattern.

Women of all ages act as if money is a complicated "thing" to master. Something better left to "experts" or a male figure in their lives. They often become the helpless traveler in their financial lives.

A husband, boyfriend, dad or well-meaning friend charts their financial course. The person seems to be "competent" at money or, at the very least, interested in the subject.

What does it mean to be financially empowered?

Taking responsibility and control of your money is one big step to feeling empowered. The definition of empowerment is compelling: the process of becoming stronger and more confident, especially in controlling one's life and claiming one's rights. (3)

Back to my story: I went to work on the third day after that terrifying morning in the lawyer's boardroom and presented a complicated project status report to our CEO. I competently answered her questions, gave forecasts and important facts. As the Program Director, I had a firm handle on ALL the details of my multi-million and complicated project. If I hadn't, it would not be long before I was replaced. I presented well, answered tough questions, and the meeting ended without incident. I left the office to keep my second appointment that day with a local bank manager.

I went to the small branch and was shown the office where we would be taking care of a very simple transaction: opening up a checking account. That's when the stuff hit the fan.

"What kind of account do you need?" she asked as she brought me a cup of coffee. I began to get very anxious because I had not had to take care of any banking for over 20 years.

"A checking account, I think." I stammered.

She asked if I needed help with investments or credit cards. At this point, the tears began to flow. She looked at me with a surprised face—where was the put together, large and "in charge" woman that had walked in just moments before? I was staring out the window, wiping tears from my eyes. No matter what I did, I could not control the tears.

"I don't know exactly what I need . . . I guess a credit card and maybe a money market account. I'm not sure." I was lost. My husband had taken care of everything to do with money for over 20 years. I had had a debit card and a joint credit card in my wallet and not a care in the financial world for decades. Now I had to figure out what I needed, and I didn't even know where to begin.

Suze Orman, the famous New York Times best selling author of *Women and Money*, twice named to the Time 100 and ranked among the World's 100 Most Powerful Women by Forbes, says this in her book: "Why is it that women who are so competent in all other areas of their lives cannot find the same competence when it comes to matters of money?"

Ouch. It was happening to me.

This story repeats itself every day, to thousands of women in our country. I was one of the lucky ones because our divorce had not left me in a financial mess. Many women are left with debt they knew nothing about and other financial obligations. I just had to figure out my financial life—along with everything else. **More often than not, we have no one to blame but ourselves for being in this predicament, for agreeing to remain a "helpless traveler."**

We've been busy, distracted, told that "money is complicated" or "don't worry your pretty head with those things" or "you're not good at math—let someone else do it". The list of things we have been either told or adopted is endless. And we have allowed those beliefs to govern our financial lives.

Some of us willingly participated in the giving away of our financial knowledge, and with it, our financial power.

We have to take back the intellectual management of our money and be in control of our future. If we give someone control over our money, it needs to be done with careful thought. We must hold ourselves accountable for understanding money, how it grows, how it flows, how we can make more of it and how we can safeguard it. We need to know how much we need to retire comfortably and have a plan to acquire what is needed.

Some of you reading this are saying, "You're over reacting, Diana. Sorry that happened to you, but I am fine."

You can choose to be empowered or give away your financial power—that choice is always yours. I am convinced we women need to build a new relationship with money. In preparation for this book, I scoured the medical literature for evidence that men were biologically better endowed to manage money. They are not. They are, on average, bigger and stronger than the average female living on this planet. But their brains have no more evolved "areas" than women.

If you are not financially empowered, I am here to tell you it's not entirely your fault. What you learned about money as a child is likely running your financial life RIGHT NOW. The school system didn't do much to help change that, either. Most schools did not offer classes on budgeting, finance or money management. Young adults have very few savvy financial models to emulate, either.

Where do we begin? May I suggest the same place I began: get knowledge.

Buy at least four books on the basics of financial management. My personal journey began with *Women and Money* by Suze Orman, *Smart Women Finish Rich* by David Bach, *The Total Money Makeover* by Dave Ramsey and the classic *Rich Dad Poor Dad* by Robert Kiyosaki.

The most important part of reading the books is DOING what they tell you to do. The first three give you specific actions to take. DO THEM. Just like reading about exercising will not increase your muscle mass, reading about money without taking steps will not help, either. Create your net-worth statement, put together the budget, and make an appointment with a financial advisor. I went to my bank's website and looked at their Wealth Management Services. From there, I choose an advisor and made an appointment. **Come with an open mind and take notes. You do not have to follow every single piece of advice they give you. Remember, YOU are now in charge.** Listen to what they advise and do your own research. Do not hesitate to find another advisor in another institution and make another appointment. Remember, they are there to serve YOU. Their job is to put together a plan and help you.

Listen to what I am saying next: REGARDLESS of how much money you have, start this process. You may have assets or not. You may be financially "in the hole"—START THE PROCESS.

The next step for me was talking to two or three financially successful friends or relatives. Find a friend that seems to be financially informed. Ask them if they have a plan. If they do, ask if they will kindly share their best advice. Word of caution: don't feel the need to share your financial particulars. No one needs to know your credit score or how much debt or money you have. Sharing these details may make you feel vulnerable. We don't need that at this particular juncture of our financial journey. Ask them what they have done that they are most happy about and what are the two things you should avoid doing. Write down what they say and put it in your knowledge base.

Next Step: Create Your Life Plan

I have met very few people who have a plan for their lives. Most are passive spectators, watching their lives unfold a day at a time. They may plan their careers, the building of a new home, or even a vacation. But it never occurs to them to plan their life. As a result, many end up discouraged and disillusioned, wondering where they went wrong. As a coach, I have found that the majority of people have "generic goals" for their lives, such as "be happy" or "have money" or "be healthy." Very few take the time to write down their specific ideal life and then put a plan together to achieve that Life Plan.

My Life Plan includes the following sections: God, my family, my home, my health, my career and my money. Each of these sections describes in detail how I want my life to look. For example, under Health, I have written, "My body is lean and strong. I run 4 times a week and do strength training twice a week. I eat solely plant-based meals four days a week. I make yearly appointments with my physician for physicals, mammograms and health related blood work. I am up to date on all recommended procedures such as colonoscopies."

Be specific about what you want your life to look like. It's ok to want what you want. It's YOUR life. I review my Life Plan several times a year. I lovingly update it and keep adding details to it.

Last Step: Create Your Loose-Ends List

I created a list of all the "loose ends" in my life at that point. Some were big items like "get an estate plan (will)." Others were "cancel this credit card or monthly subscription." This is not a daily activity list that contains things like "clean out the garage" or "go to the gym." I wrote down a list of things that needed to be done to ensure my life was "tidy." It may sound morbid, but I visualized my oldest child having to dig through my life to take care of my final wishes. I wanted to provide him a binder with everything in it completely up to date. After all, I was now divorced and didn't have someone who could do it. I wanted my son to be impressed with his mom and how she had managed her affairs.

I set a goal to clear up the entire list in six months. Some were easy: a phone call and it was done. Others involved going to the courthouse to change the name on important documents—a more complicated process for sure, but one that needed to be done. The day I crossed off the last item on my Loose Ends list, I sat back, and the most amazing feeling came over me: "I am a grown-up now. I am empowered over all aspects of my life. I don't have millions of dollars or properties scattered all over the world (yet), but what I do have is in good shape, accounted for and documented."

Empowerment. Peace.

In the spirit of full disclosure, I want you to know that after three years of being divorced and not speaking to one another, my ex-husband and I met over a glass of wine and blessed one another with love and forgiveness. We had both grown substantially from the divorce and had chosen to make more of our respective lives. We had become better people in every aspect. We were humble towards each other and grateful for the 22 years we had had together. It was a tender and healing moment for both of us. He later confided that he had been impressed with how I had managed myself. He looked around at the home I had bought on my own, how I had invested my money and the lack of loose ends—and he was impressed.

It opened a door to a better and renewed relationship. We began to see that we had never stopped loving one another and that we wanted to try again—this time from a different place in our hearts and minds. We re-married and are incredibly happy. Things between us are better than ever before, but one thing I kept from my financial empowerment journey: I manage my own money. It is not a trust thing. I hide nothing and neither does he. I just know that I need to manage my money for my own sake.

And it feels very empowering.

Recommended Book Reading List:

Orman, S. (2007). *Women & Money: Owning the Power to Control Your Destiny*. United States: Random House Publishing Group.

Ramsey, Dave. *The Total Money Makeover: A Proven Plan for Financial Fitness*. United States, Thomas Nelson, 2003.

Smart Women Finish Rich: 9 Steps to Achieving Financial Security and Funding Your Dreams by David Bach, illustrated edition, Doubleday Canada, 2003, ISBN: 0385659679, 9780385659673

Rich Dad, Poor Dad by Robert T. Kiyosaki, Lulu Press, Inc 2016, ISBN: 1365076350, 9781365076350

----

(1) The 6 Nasty Financial Surprises For Divorcing Women, Forbes On-line Magazine **By Laurie Itkin**, Next Avenue **Contributor** July 15, 2018
(2) www.yourdivorcequestions.org/how-will-divorce-affect-me-financially/
(3) www.dictionary.com

Diana Miret

Diana Miret is the Numbers Whisperer. She can tell a business owner's story just by looking at their numbers. She developed this superpower after years of studies and skilled training. She is the recipient of a BA in Accounting and Finance and spent several quarters on the Dean's List at the University of Cincinnati. She is an MIT certified Process Master and holds a green belt in Six Sigma and Lean Sigma. And as with most superheroes, they use their superpowers for good. And that is what Diana has set out to do with her coaching practice—The Business Profit Coach, LLC.

With her combined 35+ years as a corporate executive at companies ranging from banks in Canada to a Dot com, Diana is leveraging her expertise in project management, planning and business profitability to help business owners stay in business.

Her clients are varied, but the one thing they have in common is that, to them, cash is not a bad four-letter word. Diana is set apart from most other business coaches in that she is also a certified life coach and uses this skill to uncover emotional and relation issues with money that often is the catalyst of poor money management.

She is a highly sought-after speaker on this topic and has been interviewed by the Treasure Coast Connector and appeared on iHeart Radio.

Diana is an avid runner. She is currently training for her 11th marathon in March 2020 in Barcelona, Spain.

Social Media Links:
Email address: diana@dianamiret.com
Phone Number: 772-497-4645
Website: www.dianamiret.com
Facebook page: https://www.facebook.com/BusinessProfitCoaching/
LinkedIn: www.linkedin.com/dianamiret

GROW YOUR BUSINESS
BY REBECCA HALL GRUYTER

"Every problem is a gift – without problems we would not grow."
~Tony Robbins

I believe your work can be your passion and your heart; it taps into your deepest talents and purpose, and you feel blessed to be allowed to do this for a living! Your business is all you dreamed it would be, and you enjoy hopping out of bed (at least most mornings) to go to work and serve as you are called.

And then . . . what felt like ease begins to feel like effort. You find yourself in catch-up mode, running here and there to put out fires or fill in where someone has dropped the ball. You are attracting more people, which is exciting and what you wanted, yet you are so busy meeting everyone's needs that you're beginning to get . . . tired.

Learning #1: Recognizing the difference between *true growth* and a *busy season*

There are times when you realize that you're really, really busy, which is usually a good thing! It is very important to be aware of what is actually going on: Is this just a busy season, or is your business having a growth spurt? Or is it true, sustainable growth?

Why is this important? When you're in the middle of busyness it is easy to get so caught up in the immediate, everyday dealings that you don't look ahead. You push and push, add extra help when you need it, and can often fill in the gaps yourself.

You know, we women are good at filling in the gaps to get things done, aren't we?

I found myself in this position last fall when we had one exciting book launch after another. My team was working hard, we were doing great things, I personally was pushing, pushing, doing, doing. At one point, one of my team members had to step away at a critical time, and I happily stepped in to fill that gap to monitor a book launch (I think I got two hours of sleep that night!).

This was fine, for a while. But I began to realize that something "new" was happening: Our business was moving in a direction that wasn't just about a busy season – it was about true growth. There didn't seem to be an end in sight for my "filling in the gaps," and I was bringing people on to do more and more things for longer periods of time.

Here is what happens with the "busy season" mindset: You keep plugging along and often forget marketing to invite new business. You risk making commitments you can't keep, especially with the people you've hired and brought with you. You discover that you always put yourself in the position of filling the gap, and you are feeling exhausted and your energy is deflating. The team keeps pushing forth using the same systems and programs that aren't meeting your goals anymore.

When you recognize that this may be a growth step – how exciting! – then it's time to pull back from the weeds. It's time to step back and look at:

- What are we building?
- What is our purpose now? Our focus? Our mission?
- What actions do we need to take?
- What do I need to delegate?
- What are the high-level decisions that I need to make?
- What do we as an organization no longer need to do?
- How do we build our teams for sustainable growth?
- How can we become more scalable?
- How can we cross train more so the leader isn't stepping in to fill the gaps all the time?
- Where is our true place in in the market(s) we serve? Has it changed from before? Where is it now and do we need to align or shift anything to serve if better?

Then you can begin to get strategic about your direction, delegating and hiring, and adjusting programs and systems that will meet your new growth goals. What I have found is that you really can't move forward with these important growth strategies UNTIL you recognize exactly where your business stands.

Learning #2: Taking care of your team and your team's needs

I know you, as an empowered woman, care about your team and that they care about you and your shared vision. You all pull together when it's needed, during those busy seasons and when those projects come up that need everyone's heart and hands.

A team that really cares is so important. I often get messages from people about my team, such as how responsive they are and how passionate they are about what we're doing. It fills my heart, and I appreciate them very much. I try to make sure that I express my appreciation and gratitude to them whenever I can.

A caring team becomes so much more important when you are going through a growth spurt. Changes, uncertainties, and new things to learn are all part of a growth experience. You want your team to be ready to adapt to the changes and, in fact, to be part of creating them! There are several ways to bring your team along with you on the growth path, and of course keep the caring going as you add new hires to the team.

1. **Cross-train skill sets.** You are probably not the only one who's filling in gaps. The team can get stretched and might be filling in where they are not feeling comfortable or familiar with the task they are being asked to do. One solution we've found is starting to cross-train in different skill sets, so that more than one person knows how to do a certain task and we can fill in for each other to accomplish it.

2. **Help your team speak the same language.** Especially when we are working with clients, we want to make sure they always feel our "brand," our core values, and our service to them. As you grow, the customer face can't always be the leader, so it's up to you to share your "language" with your team members. It's also called organizational culture, which I define as the underlying beliefs, values, and ways of interacting with people inside and outside the organization.

3. **Help your team understand their roles — and yours.** When your business is smaller, your people come to you directly for lots of things. If a customer has a question or issue, your team might send them directly to you, the leader. But in order to grow, your team needs to take on more responsibility for making decisions on their own. Train them to know what to do when they don't know what to do. They don't have to have all the answers, and you don't have to be available 24/7 to provide them! This is important so you aren't a "gap filler."
   Remember you have a team to support you . . . so that you can serve and support your customers. It doesn't always have to be you. We have developed a go-to phrase our people can use to respond to customers in a way that serves them while allowing the time for the right person to provide the right answer to them. This way we are being responsive and caring while not setting the expectation that the leader of the company will stop everything to personally handle every issue.

4. **Delegate, and trust.** Once you have taught your team these skills, it's time to allow them to take the authority to do their job, and to trust them to do it. During this process, encourage them and receive their feedback and ideas. At the same time, watch for the warning signs that things might not be going as expected, and follow up on the issues to address any problems. Make sure you take care of these while the

warning signs are cautionary yellow, and not allow them to get to flashing red!

5. **Reinforce roles.** It is important to support your team and not undermine them and their authority. If a customer or client comes to you directly to handle something or to "override" a team member or to "skip steps" . . . be careful how you choose to handle this situation when it happens. Look for ways to kindly reinforce that team member's role. Let the client know they are in great hands with your team member and redirect them to the appropriate person that can handle their issue. Let your team member handle it and only step in if needed to back them up, support them, and if needed, redirect where things need to go or another way they can/could handle the situation. Empower them . . . but do so behind the scenes. Help them grow while serving your amazing clients.

Again, train then trust your team to take delegation. If you don't trust and don't give your people a chance to perform, then you're once again filling the gaps, whether or not they need to be filled by you. And you may find yourself back where you started! And if you are constantly filling gaps, you can't lead the company. Things need to be able to continue to operate and move forward when you're out of the office. Build a self-sufficient, independent, and empowered team. A business takes time to grow, and it can be challenging to be patient. It is important to be patient with ourselves and others. The decision-making and relationship-building all take time. So, be empowered, and be patient with yourself and your team.

Learning #3: Going through your own growth realization process

Let's return to that busy season that is actually true growth. You have been in the weeds, and you now recognize that something exciting and maybe a little scary is happening to your business. You are taking some steps to move forward, putting out little fires before they become big ones, making decisions and some quick additions to your team to keep things going.

Before you go too far, take some time to step back from the weeds and think about YOU:

Look at what excites you about your business. It may involve reminding yourself of your original mission and purpose in getting into this business. You may discover something that you thought was important at the beginning but is not so important or within your focus now. Notice whether or not you would miss that thing if you released it.

Think about what keeps rising to the top for you — is it something that your customers are asking for consistently? Is it something you're feeling called to do, like speak on stage or write a book? Is it a new direction you can begin to set a vision for to achieve down the road a few months or years? Is it a shift in your role as ambassador of your brand (the "face" of the company) — are you feeling that your brand could benefit from your taking less of a customer-facing role, or a more visible role?

These are all considerations that are important to contemplate, journal about, and maybe discuss with people close to you whom you trust. It's worth the time so that you can be sure you are moving in the right direction with your growth plan.

On this exploration, you may bump up against ***how you're meant to serve.*** I have done this myself in the past, when I've found that I'm trying to fit myself in a box that I don't fit into anymore in order to serve. One way this came up for me was during an early growth spurt. I was doing a lot of personal hands-on coaching, plus hosting large events, my own radio and TV programs, and expanding my business to publishing and broader visibility networks. As I continued to serve more people — happily! — I was getting stretched thinner and thinner. I was involving myself personally in everything, including physically assembling each event program!

I couldn't be everywhere at once and answer every individual's needs at every moment (as the "individuals" expanded to many thousands all over the world) — but, believe me, I tried! Finally, after many inner conversations and prayer, I came to this realization: I could still authentically and lovingly reach more people with my gifts in ways that spotlight others to take the lead, allow my team to take a greater part in our success, and find the most effective and fulfilling ways to focus my time and gifts. Now, I still do have personal interactions and relationships with my clients, but they are in areas where I'm most called to serve.

Once you have gone through your growth realization process, what's next? More questions and reflections! They should be easier to answer now because you are in a better position than ever to discover new ways to serve, to touch the lives of others. You may be coming out of hiding to a more expanded level of visibility and service, evolving to a next step to fulfill your calling to make a difference in others' lives!

You are saying "yes" to these new opportunities, knowing that your plans and strategies will flow with ease because you are clear on what your vision is, what you want to lead, and in what direction your business is headed.

Next-step considerations:

1. Ask yourself: What is my role now?
2. Determine where your time is best spent now in terms of growing this business and handling your team.
3. Open yourself to attract the people you can really help, who are ready and willing to put "skin in the game" to receive your form of transformation!
4. Build the "people resources" you need to create your action plan: your team, of course, looking for the right people to help you, and also coaches, mentors, friends, and experts to support you in taking your vision to the next level.
5. Begin to look at the systems you're using now, and how you and your team can ensure that they will support your next stage of growth.

Then you will be ready to choose your path to SHINE as an empowered woman, grow your business, reach more people and serve with your organization supporting people around the world in a sustainable way! The world needs more of you and all that you have to offer. Be willing to grow and grow your business to reach and serve more people.

Rebecca Hall Gruyter

Rebecca Hall Gruyter is an Influencer and Empowerment Leader committed to bringing Experts and Influencers forward so that together we can lean in and make the world a better place, one heart and life at a time. She is the owner of *Your Purpose Driven Practice*, creator of the *Women's Empowerment Series* events/TV show, the *Speaker Talent Search*™, and *Your Success Formula*™. Rebecca is an in-demand speaker, an expert money coach, and a frequent guest expert on success panels, tele-summits, TV, and radio shows. Rebecca specializes in using her over 10 million promotional reach to help you be seen, heard, and SHINE!

As the CEO of *RHG Media Productions*™, Rebecca launched the international TV Network (www.RHGTVNetwork.com) to bring even more positive and transformational programming to the world. In July 2017, she launched the Global RHG Magazine & TV Guide, bringing inspirational influences to the world and their messages! In January 2018, she expanded RHG Publishing to now help individual authors bring their books forward as bestsellers so they can be positioned as they bring their powerful books forward.

Rebecca is a popular and syndicated radio talk show host, #1 bestselling author (multiple times), and publisher who wants to help YOU impact the world powerfully!

Rebecca@YourPurposeDrivenPractice.com
www.facebook.com/rhallgruyter (Facebook)
www.YourPurposeDrivenPractice.com (Main Website)
www.RHGTVNetwork.com (TV Network)
www.SpeakerTalentSearch.com (Free Opportunity for Speakers to get on More Stages)
www.EmpoweringWomenTransformingLives.com (Weekly Radio Show)
www.MeetWithRebecca.com (Calendar link to schedule a time to talk with Rebecca)

THE POWER OF PERSISTENCE, QUESTIONS AND ALIGNMENT OF PURPOSE

BY WENDY K. BENSON AND ELIZABETH A. MYERS

What do Wendy Benson and Elizabeth (Beth) Myers have in common? They are both powerful leaders of an organization leading teams of experts who help fill the gaps that can sometimes occur in the healthcare industry and are #1 International Best-Selling Authors. They have discovered the power of persistence and alignment of purpose as the keys to living in an empowered way. Beth grew up in the southern suburbs of Chicago and Wendy Benson was raised in a rural area of northwestern Pennsylvania. One spent her summers going to Major League Baseball games and the other went camping in the woods of northern Canada. Beth never stopped moving as a child, so she became a gymnast. Wendy loved reading as a summer past-time, although some of that can be attributed to there not being a television in her home. While many of their experiences are different, their approach to life is in complete alignment: they are both committed to caring for others—with compassion and with persistence.

Beth and Wendy were both young adults when they had loved ones who were diagnosed with cancer: Beth's niece and Wendy's mother. Beth's niece was diagnosed with leukemia and needed aggressive treatment and a number of hospitalizations. Wendy's mother was diagnosed with breast cancer and went through surgery, chemotherapy, radiation, and intensive care. Because of these experiences, they were both forever changed. Even though they both have clinical backgrounds (Beth is a nurse and Wendy is an occupational therapist), they never viewed healthcare, or being a patient, the same after that. **For Beth and Wendy, there is true power in being persistent: the power of asking questions and the power of being invested as a patient, family member, leader, and person.**

How can each of us embrace our power of persistence? How does being persistent help us and those we care about? In their professional lives, and in their personal ones, Wendy and Beth have discovered persistence is a critical key to helping to support and reassure others. Beth founded the company 2x2 Health: Private Health Concierge because she witnessed a need that often was not being met in healthcare. Patients can feel overwhelmed, may not know where to turn or who to ask for help and support—and both Beth and Wendy knew exactly what that feels like. Wendy joined Beth at 2x2 Health, and together, they have built a multidisciplinary team of experts who fill in the gaps that sometimes can occur in healthcare. **Wendy and Beth, as healthcare professionals and business leaders, have identified the following four important strategies for utilizing persistence to achieving optimal results and feeling confident. These strategies are applicable not only when focusing on your health or that of a loved one, but also when you are focusing on optimizing your life overall.**

Key Persistence Strategies:

1. **Ask Questions**
2. **Know (or Get to Know) Yourself**
3. **Prepare in Advance, Make a Plan—Even if it Changes**
4. **Develop and Maintain Connections**

Strategy 1—Ask Questions for Increased Understanding

Although both Beth and Wendy are healthcare professionals, they came to embrace the field of healthcare in their own unique way. Beth knew she wanted to be a nurse as a young child; Wendy did not know that healthcare and occupational therapy were her professional passion until she volunteered at a hospital during her college years. A common thread in academic medicine is asking "why?" In any professional industry and throughout life, it is important to be proactive in your learning, which leads to an increased understanding. An ideal way to do this is by asking questions. **Beth and Wendy strongly agree on the value of asking questions**—whether you are caring for your aging parent, collaborating with your child's teacher, or exploring promotional opportunities at your job. When we ask questions, we are showing others that we are invested in learning more, that we have the desire to expand our current awareness, and that we are motivated to increase our knowledge base. There may be times when you do not even know where to start with a complex situation and their experience is that open-ended questions are an effective tool to learn more about any given topic.

Examples of questions include:

a. **For an aging parent when you are trying to find out how they are feeling/doing:**
"What did you enjoy doing today?"
"What are your biggest challenges?"
"Are there parts of your daily routine that make you nervous?"
"Tell me a little more about your plans for this week."
"Is there something on your schedule coming up you are looking forward to?"
"Are there situations that are stressful for you?"

b. **For collaborating with a childcare provider or teacher:**
"Can you tell me more about what you think is going well for my child and areas where there are opportunities for continued focus?"
"What are activities that you are doing in class that we can help to continue to work on at home?"
"What are your primary priorities and how can we work together to enhance my child's development?"

c. **For focusing on enhancing professional development:**
"I am motivated to continue to contribute to this organization. Are there ways that I can do that at a higher level?"

"Can you tell me more about ways that others have expanded their responsibilities here (this department/this organization)?"
"What are the most important priorities of this job and what demonstrates success?"

There are times that, even when questions are asked, you may not get the information that you need. At this point, persistence is the key. Perhaps a question can be asked in a different way, or maybe you need to ask a different person. When you have tried to get answers and are unsuccessful, try asking, "I'm really curious about this; can you tell me more?"

Strategy 2—Know (or Get to Know) Yourself

Do you seek out time with other people or do you prefer to re-charge by having some time on your own? Taking the time to be introspective on what works the best for YOU is well worth the time. Beth's husband is a surgeon, and she laughingly shares that she has a short window of time to communicate the most important facts with him—about two minutes. There are others who prefer to spend more time and energy to talk through a process and various options. It can be helpful to know who in your social network you can reach out to depending on your needs. Wendy's husband travels regularly for work, and she has learned to plan social outings during some of the evenings that he is gone so that when he returns home, she doesn't expect him to be energized to go to a restaurant for a family dinner. That way, her social needs are met, and when he returns, they can relax at home with their daughters. As you take the time to think through what works well for you, **it is important to understand that there is not a "right or wrong" or a "good or bad" answer. The true power comes from knowing what works well for each of us individually so that we can consistently perform at our own personal highest level.**

Some questions and thoughts to determine what works well for you as an individual:

a. Do you crave more time with other people or do you feel more centered when you've had individual, quiet time?

b. Are you a person who prefers agreement or do you like to "debate" during discussions?
c. Do you like to plan in advance for activities or do you enjoy spontaneity?
d. Do you prefer quiet, reflective walks or hard-core work outs with loud music?
e. Are you an independent worker or do you like to collaborate with others on projects?

When we better understand ourselves and our preferences, we can better arrange our environments to match our tendencies. Do you like a quiet environment to work in or do you concentrate better if there is conversation and music in the background? If your workspace is busier and louder than you prefer, maybe earplugs can help. Do you need more socialization than your professional and personal life is currently providing? Perhaps joining a book club would be a great fit. It is also interesting to note that these preferences can shift over time when your life changes. For Wendy, after she became a mother of two daughters, even though being socially active continued to be important to her, she had to purposefully rearrange her schedule to allow time for the additional responsibilities that come with being a parent. In her situation, joining a "mom's group" that included play time for the kids and visiting time for the parents was an effective way to meet her needs.

Strategy #3—Prepare in Advance, Make a Plan—Even if it Changes

As business owners, mothers, wives, and active members in the community, Beth and Wendy place a very high priority on planning and preparing in advance. This is often not easy to do, but structure can make seemingly overwhelming tasks much more manageable. Whether you use your daily calendar as your guide or are a spreadsheet junkie, knowing the overall goal and the steps to take can make a real difference—both in your ability to accomplish your priorities as well as to decrease your stress level.

Questions/steps to make a plan, even if it is on a trial basis:

a. **Identify your overall goal.** Perhaps you are interested in a job change. An overall goal in this example could be to secure employment with a role in an organization that values your skills and talents.

b. **List and prioritize steps to achieve your goal**. Using the example of the job change, ways that one could identify important tactics include: consider industry and position interests, update resume to align with ideal positions, research job search mechanisms, sign up for job notifications, identify, review, and practice potential interview questions.

c. **Identify persons/processes that need to be included.** As you continue to plan for your job change, are there leaders or former colleagues in the industry who would be helpful for you to reach out to? Also, this is the ideal time to connect with those you would like to be your references to share with them your plans and to solicit their feedback on your search.

d. **Complete the steps.** As you make progress on completing your steps, document your accomplishments, add dates and any follow up comments. Not only can this be helpful to monitor and track your progress, but for many people, also seeing the action taken and steps completed along the way can be motivating. There are times when regularly following up and communicating with a family member or friend can help keep you accountable, especially if you start to lose momentum. As you continue your progress with various tasks toward your primary goal, be sure to take the time to acknowledge your hard work and to celebrate your accomplishments.

e. **Reevaluate the steps.** Depending on the overall goal, there are times when we need to reassess our proposed next steps and adjust our course of action accordingly. For the job seeking example, you may find that you do not need to reach out to multiple industry leaders if an ideal opportunity presents itself early in the process. There also can be changes to the timing of the goal or unanticipated geographical considerations depending on your ideal role and leads for potential employers.

Preparing a plan in advance and following through with your primary goal takes persistence—and it is well worth it. If your goal is important enough for you to identify and spend your time thinking about it, then it is important enough to build a plan for it. Taking time to plan for your objective helps you effectively manage the process and significantly increases the likelihood of you achieving your goal.

Strategy 4—Maintaining and creating connections

Having connections is essential in all the stages of our lives. Beth lives relatively close to many of her family members and values spending time with them. Because Wendy does not have family in the Chicagoland area, she relies on technology to stay in touch with family in Pennsylvania and has "adopted" her family and community support with her in-laws as well as very close friends and neighbors. Researchers agree, our connections are important at any age, but they can be even more critical when we are going though significant changes in our lives: changes in relationships, having children—or having them move away for college or jobs—balancing professional and personal priorities, and taking care of others in addition to ourselves. **The following are key takeaways that have helped Beth and Wendy and others they frequently interact with, both professionally and personally:**

a. **Take time to identify**—who is "on your team"? As our friend and colleague Dr. Kathy Tynus shared with us, "You can't choose what you are going through, but you can choose who you have on this journey with you, who is in your community of support."

b. **When in time of significant change, are there activities that you can outsource to, or share with, others?** Carpooling, childcare, meal preparation or delivery, grocery or pharmacy store runs, pet care, etc.

c. **Actively engage with and build rapport with those in your community.** Are there some people you would like to get to know better or activities you'd like to focus on? Make it a priority and follow up on these priorities with a written plan if that is helpful for you. This is an ideal way to use your persistence to make a significant, positive difference in your life.

d. **Familiarize yourself with regional or national organizations who can be a resource, either right away or in the future.** Some choose to do independent on-line research and you can also reach out to your current network to learn more about the organizations who have been helpful for others.

e. **Take good care of yourself by making connections with others and being especially kind to yourself:**

- o Do or watch something that makes you laugh
- o Engage with others, especially in a way that has meaning
- o Discuss what is important to you with someone you trust
- o Take time to celebrate along the way. It is not only helpful to have someone to connect with when you need support, but it is also important to have someone to talk with when you are celebrating the special moments in your life.

Beth and Wendy are honored to share their experience and perspective with you and are grateful for your time. Throughout their personal and professional lives, persistence has been a common thread throughout their journeys. They attribute persistence, asking productive questions, and an alignment of purpose as key contributors to their success. When you choose to focus on these, you will be better positioned to have significant accomplishments with your professional growth and with your personal fulfillment. Being curious to learn more and investing in the process of educating yourself and others gives you additional power; it strengthens your knowledge. With increased knowledge, your alignment of purpose is motivating and achievable. Persistence, asking questions, and having a strong alignment of purpose, are incredibly powerful traits to cultivate and we all have this capability within our control. You've definitely got this; you can do it. Unleash the power of your inner-persistence, your curiosity, and your alignment of purpose today!

Wendy K. Benson and Elizabeth (Beth) A. Meyers

Wendy K. Benson is a healthcare executive, occupational therapist and partner at 2×2 Health: Private Health Concierge. Wendy views healthcare through a unique lens, combining both her executive leadership and clinical perspectives. She managed the day-to-day operations of multiple service lines at a residential neurological center, a level one inner city trauma hospital, and a tertiary care academic medical center. Wendy mentors emerging healthcare leaders and is a faculty member of the Master of Science in Health Systems Management Program at Rush University where she serves on the Admissions Committee and as a Faculty Advisor. She is a member of Greater National Advocates, Greater Chicago Advocates and is a board member of The Woman's Board of Rush University Medical Center, Greenlight Family Services, and Friends of Blaine.

Elizabeth (Beth) A. Myers is a registered nurse and founder of 2×2 Health: Private Health Concierge. Throughout her career, Beth understood the frustration of patients and their families, not knowing where to turn or how to navigate the healthcare system. Beth spent two decades in clinical, research, and patient safety roles, including serving as the past president of nursing staff, transplant coordinator, and transplant clinical nurse manager. She served as a pediatric intensive care unit critical care nurse and worked as a bariatric nurse coordinator. Beth is a member of Sigma Theta Tau, Greater Chicago Advocates and the Greater National Advocates, and serves as a board member of Greenlight Family Services and The Woman's Board of Rush University Medical Center.

Email Addresses:
wbenson@2x2health.com
bmyers@2x2health.com
Phone Number:
(833) 2x2-NURS
(833) 292-6773
Website:
http://2x2health.com/
Facebook:
https://www.facebook.com/2x2health/
Linked In Page:
https://www.linkedin.com/company/2x2-health-private-health-concierge-llc/?viewAsMember=true

FAITH + ACTION = EMPOWERED
BY FAITH JAMES

The greatest con is the myth that women are weak and lack the competence to manage power. And unwittingly, most women have blindly adopted this notion and passed down this fallacy through generations. **In order for women to regain strong footing and stand in our own power, we have to stop believing this lie and tap into the truth of what God says about us.**

Here's the simple fact: to be empowered, you must stand in the truth of what God says about you. Choose to believe this, and reject everything else. So how do you do that in the face of a tsunami of negative self-talk and judgment and criticism of others? You keep your eyes and ears focused on the words of God.

"I praise you because I am fearfully and wonderfully made; your works are wonderful; I know that full well."
- *Psalm* 139:14

Let's deconstruct the above scripture to learn how to do focus on His words.

There are three key sections:

1. **The action** (praising God);
2. **The why** (being fearfully and wonderfully made);
3. **The acknowledgement** (I know that full well).

To be empowered, you have to praise God continually for the gift of your life and your purpose here in the world. Your acknowledgement of the fact that your life is a miracle is central to being empowered. Then you must affirm that you know this to be true. Affirm that you know you are a miracle. Affirm that you know you are fearfully and wonderfully made. Affirm that you know it fully well. This is your unshakeable knowing.

"No one can make you feel inferior without your consent."
- Eleanor Roosevelt

The Grass is Purple and The Sky is Green

My client Debra Graugnard, a spiritual healer, uses this analogy to illustrate this point to her female clients. If someone told you the sky is green and the grass is purple, your reaction would be that this person is a bit off. You wouldn't go shrieking in horror that you had been wrong all along thinking that the sky was blue and the grass is green. Why? Because you know full well that the sky is blue and the grass is green. You see it every day with your own eyes.

Yet, when someone says you're not worthy or valuable, women tend to believe those negative notions and shrink into their shells. This is something we must reject swiftly.

"Be strong and take heart, and have no fear of them: for it is the Lord your God who is going with you; he will not take away his help from you." - Deuteronomy 31:6

You Gotta Have Faith

When I came into the world, I was in full-blown trauma. Actually, I was in trauma before I came into this world. My mother had an abusive relationship with my father when she was 7 months pregnant with me, and my father and the woman he was having an affair with physically beat my mom. When I was born, I weighed only 6.5 pounds and could not breathe. I was like a fish out of water gulping for air. The nurse rushed me to ICU where I stayed for two days fighting for my life. My mom was left alone in her hospital room with only her thoughts and God observing her . . . waiting for her to speak to Him. During her pregnancy, she had wished that she would lose the pregnancy because of the physical abuse she suffered by my father. She pleaded with God to miscarry because she hated her husband. But when she saw me, she wanted her baby to live. God heard her prayers and obliged. As a result, she named me Faith. By naming me Faith, she committed my life to honor God for answering her prayers. She would tell me that story often, and from an early age I have known that God approved me and saved my life for me to complete His purpose for me.

This is how you should see yourself. That fact that you are alive is proof that God also approved you and wants you to complete His purpose for your life. I want every woman to see herself as special, appointed and worthy. We are all here for a purpose.

The Answer To Any Question is Faith

Faith!! This is the secret ingredient to being empowered. Bar none, this has been the secret to my success in personal life and business. It sounds simple and it is. You have to have faith in God that He can do what He says He will do. When you have faith, even faith as small as a mustard seed, you build up your confidence and your confidence leads you down the path of empowerment.

Fearless, Faith-filled Females

Often times we need to see people modeling the desired behavior to give us that initial push into the right direction. Let these Fearless, Faith-filled Females of the Bible serve as your guide.

Sarah went from being barren to becoming the Mother of Nations.

Sarah, the then 80-year old wife of Abraham, was chosen by God for greatness. She was told that God selected her to become the mother of nations and to have Kings in her lineage by giving birth to a son with her husband Abraham, who was 100 years old. But Sarah's vision of herself was tamped down by limiting beliefs and she scoffed and laughed at God. But, God's word being truth, she in fact bore Abraham a son. ***Sarah then demonstrated her faith by leaving her comfortable home and embarked on the journey that God laid out for her to in fact become the mother of nations.***

Ruth went from working in the fields to owning the fields.

She was a widow from an enemy nation with no prospects. Yet, God moves so mightily in her story and uses it to encourage millions. At the beginning of the book, Ruth is living in her home in Moab, a place and people that the Israelites frowned upon. On top of that, she had lost her husband and was living with her widowed mother-in-law. She also lost her husband without a child, some believing she may have been barren. The pain Ruth must have been in was immense, but she didn't allow her past to hold her back. She had the ***faith to believe that God was who He said He was and faith to believe that God would provide for her and Naomi.*** Her bravery, faith and obedience can encourage us to be better followers of Christ. Ruth was able to overcome her past by giving her life over to the living God. By having faith in God, she was able to be used mightily by the Lord and became the great grandmother of King David.

Hannah went from being mocked for not being able to bear children to being the mother to one of the most influential-figures in the Bible.

Hannah wanted a child so badly but was infertile. She prayed to God that she would be able to have a son and in turn, promised to dedicate his life to the service of God. She gave birth to a son, named him Samuel and didn't fall short on her promise. She dedicated her baby Samuel to the Lord and left him at the temple to serve God "all the days of his life" (1 Samuel 1:11). Her son later grew up to be one of the most influential and Godly figures in the Bible. One of the most inspiring things about Hannah is the fact that she never gave up hope that God would hear her prayer. Her big faith in God and persistent prayer got God's attention. ***She believed that God would give her a son, and He multiplied her faith by giving her many children.***

The Beginning of My Journey to Faith

In 2006, my life was great! I had a six-figure corporate advertising job and traveled to fabulous places across the country and the world. I built a 5,000 sq. foot, lake-front home with a pool, furnished with high-end furniture and expensive artworks. I hosted fabulous parties for my friends and colleagues. All was going swell until the 2008 recession. I was laid off, and that lavish house became a noose around my neck.

My bills were piling up and my savings were going down. I knew I had to lease my home because I could no longer afford the carrying costs. I knew the leasing agent that I wanted to use to put it on corporate leasing, but I could not find his contact info. The following Sunday, I woke up unusually early and was flipping around the TV stations and came across a station that had sermons that so moved me that I made a donation of $25 to each ministry. That small step of faith changed everything!

The following day, I found the leasing agent's info. He told me that a house of my size and price point would be on the market for at least 12 months. Nevertheless, it was my only option, so we signed the leasing contract. That night, the agent called to say he was bringing a client the next morning—but the client was a longshot because she had small children and preferred a house that was not near water. Well, my house was on a lake, with a pool and a large water feature—yet when she saw the house, she signed the paperwork to lease the house for two years!

God supernaturally closed her eyes to the water and my house was leased after being on the market for less than 24 hours—despite the market trends! That was when God got my attention and I made the decision to start looking for a church home and to build my relationship with God. The first church I visited was a United Methodist Church on Communion Sunday. I heard the pastor mention communion and I got up and made my way up to the altar. However, on my way there I realized the pastor called for the ushers who were serving communion! I was shocked, but I just stood there. And the pastor didn't say a word to me. She simply handed me the cup, and there I was serving the blood of Christ in a church I had never been to before. That moment changed my life and is the pivotal point when I knew that having faith and trusting in God for all things was the answer. It brought me into a deep relationship with God, and I have learned that having faith in the Lord is the key to everything. The Word is core to my life in both personal and business, and I am intentional about increasing my faith and reliance on God. Since that time, there have been many, many instances where relying on my faith and trusting in the Word of God have proven to be game changers in my business.

In God We Trust

In 2016, I was once again employed in a lucrative position when God started calling me to launch my own business. It was scary to walk away from my life in corporate America, leave behind the "guaranteed six-figure paycheck," but the calling was great. So instead of living in fear, I activated my faith in God and built my branding business from nothing to six-figures in three years, simply on the strength of my faith in myself and God.

I launched my business with a one-day personal branding workshop. I spent thousands of dollars to produce it and had 30+ people in attendance. But by the end of the workshop, only one person bought a package for $297. As I reflected on the day's events, I came to the proverbial fork in the road. I could go down the path that says this was a failure and to keep my corporate job that I hated, or I could go down the path that says this is evidence that someone bought something and to keep going.

I chose to follow the optimistic sentiment expressed in the movie *Dumb and Dumber*: "*So you're telling me there's a chance!*"

Yes. I knew there was a chance for me to do big things. And my faith and risk paid off. I went from that event where I only sold one $297 package to selling $9,000 packages in two years—and this is nothing short of a miracle. I attribute my success to my faith in God. Period. God shows me time and again how mightily He moves in my life, even when I take just a small step of faith in His direction.

"The only way you can consistently experience confidence, even in environments and situations you've never previously encountered, is through the power of faith. One way to develop faith and confidence is simply to practice using it." - Tony Robbins (Awaken The Giant Within)

Developing Your Faith Muscle

Developing your faith muscle requires a commitment and a level of dedication, and it starts with the Bible and getting steeped in the Word. I have daily morning devotion time where I read my Bible, I pray, I meditate, I journal and I have conversations with God. I share daily scriptures on my social media platforms and incorporate them in my personal branding coaching business, content and training.

I want to share the top three steps of my faith process with you in the hopes of inspiring you to build your own process that can serve you for life.

Step #1 - Create a Morning Routine of Reading Your Bible

To be an empowered woman, you need to be daily steeped in God's word and believe what God says about you. Get your Bible and keep it in your nightstand. You want to have it right by your bed so it's within easy reach. So now that you have your Bible handy, where do you start? Here is one option: A *Woman's Guide to Reading the Bible in a Year* available here on Amazon: https://amzn.to/33uaT1H

Step #2 - Meditate on the promises of God

We tend to give more importance to what other people say about us rather than what God says about us. To build up your faith muscle, you must meditate on God's word and believe it. There are several instances in the Bible where God makes promises we can stand on. Here are a few of my favorites:

- "But those who hope in the LORD will renew their strength. They will soar on wings like eagles; they will run and not grow weary, they will walk and not be faint." - Isaiah 40:31
- "'No weapon forged against you will prevail, and you will refute every tongue that accuses you. This is the heritage of the servants of the LORD, and this is their vindication from me,' declares the LORD." - Isaiah 54:17
- "The LORD himself goes before you and will be with you; he will never leave you nor forsake you. Do not be afraid; do not be discouraged." - Deuteronomy 31:8
- "Have I not commanded you? Be strong and courageous. Do not be afraid; do not be discouraged, for the LORD your God will be with you wherever you go." - Joshua 1:9

Step #3 - Document Your Gratitude to God

The practice of focusing on the goodness of God cannot be understated. I keep a Gratitude journal and I document things that have happened to me in both life and business so I can give all the glory to God. This step is so important. Each day, write down five things that happened that day for which you give all glory to God. Be specific—don't write generally about being grateful for your home or food, but cite specific things that happened that day. This puts you in a practice of looking closely for things for which to praise God.

"Jesus replied to them, 'Have faith in God.'"
- Mark 11:22

We can do all things through Christ who strengthens us, and you can rise up and be an empowered woman when you focus on giving God the glory. He will continually give you more things for which you can be grateful.

Faith James

Faith James is affectionately known as the Queen of Branding or the Branding Ninja, depending on what side of the street you live. She is an award-winning marketing and branding executive with over 25+ years of experience creating branding and communications campaigns for Fortune 500 companies like IBM, Microsoft, Pepsi, Mary Kay and Liberty Mutual, to name a few.

Faith is a published author, and her recent book *Ladies Power Up Your Brand* is an Amazon international #1 best seller. She has also published articles and blog content on advertising and brand development and speaks frequently at industry shows such as the Advertising Research Federation, The American Marketing Association, Career Thought Leaders Symposium and more.

She is a certified Personal and Social Branding Strategist and is the CEO of the Personal Branding Consultancy, LLC, an international branding and marketing agency that helps forward-leaning female entrepreneurs from Austria to Atlanta build a stand-out brand and improve their professional reputation in the market place. Her agency was awarded the 2019 Branding and Marketing Agency of the year in Port St. Lucie, FL.

She is the Creator of the signature branding events Branding Over Brunch Event, Branding Over Lunch Workshop, Branding Over the Internet Networking sessions and the Branding After Dark Happy Hour and Business Mixer Events.

"Branding is in my blood! It's what I do. It's what I love."

faith@faithjames.com
612-205-6526
www.faithjames.com
https://www.facebook.com/thepersonalbrandingconsultancy/
https://twitter.com/faithjames
www.youtube.com\faithjamespersonalbrandingcoach
https://www.linkedin.com/in/faithjames/
https://www.instagram.com/faithajames
https://www.facebook.com/faith.james.10420321
https://www.pinterest.com/faithajames/

CLOSING THOUGHTS

I hope you have been touched by these powerful chapters that have encouraged, equipped, and empowered you to live on purpose while standing in your power and shining powerfully! We hope you have been encouraged and empowered by these powerful women leaders who have united together to equip and empower you to SHINE! We can't wait to see you, hear from you, and celebrate you as you share the gift of you with the world! May you always choose to ***live on purpose and with great purpose.***

****

Anthologies Compiled by Rebecca Hall Gruyter:

SHINE Series (Compiled and led by Rebecca Hall Gruyter)
- ***Come out of Hiding and SHINE!*** (Book 1)
- ***Bloom Where You are Planted and SHINE!*** (Book 2)
- ***Step Forward and SHINE!*** (Book 3)

Step Into Series (Compiled and led by Rebecca Hall Gruyter)
- ***Step Into Your Brilliance!*** (Book 1)
- ***Step Into Your Brilliant Purpose!*** (Book 2)

Experts & Influencers Series (Compiled and led by Rebecca Hall Gruyter)
- ***Experts & Influencers Series: Leadership*** (Book 1)
- ***Experts & Influencers Series: Women's Empowerment*** (Book 2)

The Grandmother Legacies (Anthology Compiled by Rebecca Hall Gruyter)

The Animal Legacies (Anthology Compiled by Rebecca Hall Gruyter)

Bloom & SHINE! (365 Daily Inspiration Anthology Compiled by Rebecca Hall Gruyter)

Empowering YOU, Transforming Lives (365 Daily Inspiration Anthology Compiled by Rebecca Hall Gruyter)

Books Featuring a Chapter by Rebecca Hall Gruyter:

The 40/40 Rules, Anthology compiled by Holly Porter
Becoming Outrageously Successful, Anthology compiled by Dr. Anita Jackson
Bright Spots, Anthology compiled by Davis Creative
Catch Your Star, Anthology published by THRIVE Publishing
Discover Your Destiny, Anthology compiled by Denise Joy Thompson
I Am Beautiful, Anthology compiled by Teresa Hawley-Howard
Movers & Shakers 2020, Anthology compiled by Teresa Hawley-Howard
The Power of Our Voices, Sharing Our Story, Anthology compiled by Teresa Hawley-Howard
Real Estate Investing for Women, Anthology compiled by Moneeka Sawyer
Succeeding Against All Odds, Anthology compiled by Sandra Yancey
Success Secrets for Today's Feminine Entrepreneurs, Anthology compiled by Dr. Anita Jackson
Unstoppable Woman of Purpose, Anthology and workbook, compiled by Nella Chikwe
Women on a Mission, Anthology compiled by Teresa Hawley-Howard
Women of Courage, Women of Destiny, Anthology compiled by Dr. Anita Jackson
Women Warriors Who Make It Rock, Anthology compiled by Nichole Peters
You Are Whole, Perfect, and Complete - Just as You Are compiled by Carol Plummer and Susan Driscoll

Journals by Rebecca Hall Gruyter:

The Animal Legacies Journal
The Experts & Influencers Leadership Journal
Women's Empowerment Journal
Step Into Your Brilliance Journal

Dear Powerful Reader,

Thank you for reading our anthology. I hope it has encouraged and empowered you and uplifted you in the area of leadership.

I wanted to share a little bit more about our organizations, Your Purpose Driven Practice™, RHG TV Network™, RHG Publishing™ and RHG Media Productions™. We are passionate about helping others live on purpose and with purpose in their life and business. I hope this book has supported and inspired you to choose to live on purpose and with great purpose in your leadership!

If you are wanting to reach more people and be part of inspiring and supporting others with your message, your gifts, and the work that you bring to the world, then I want to share some opportunities for you to consider.

Each year we compile and produce anthology book projects, support authors in publishing their own powerful books as best sellers, produce and publish an international magazine, launch TV shows, facilitate women's empowerment conferences, get quoted in major media, launch radio and podcast shows, and help experts and speakers step into a place of powerful influence to make a global difference. We provide programs and strategies to help you reach more people and facilitate the Speaker Talent Search (which helps speakers, experts, and influencers connect with more speaking opportunities). We would love to support you in reaching more people. Please take a moment to learn a little bit more about us at the sites listed below, and then reach out to us for a conversation. **We would love to help you be Seen, Heard, and SHINE!**

You can learn more about each of these things on our main website:

www.YourPurposeDrivenPractice.com
Enjoy our powerful **TV and podcast shows**: www.RHGTVNetwork.com
Learn more about the **Speaker Talent Search™:**
www.SpeakerTalentSearch.com
Learn more about our **writing opportunities**:
http://yourpurposedrivenpractice.com/writing-opportunities/

If you would like to connect with me personally to explore some of our opportunities in upcoming book projects, podcast/radio shows, and/or TV, then here is the link to schedule a time to speak with me directly: www.MeetWithRebecca.com or you can email me at: Rebecca@YourPuposeDrivenPractice.com

May you always choose to Be Seen, Heard and SHINE!

Warmly,

Rebecca Hall Gruyter

www.ingramcontent.com/pod-product-compliance
Lightning Source LLC
LaVergne TN
LVHW020636100826
845148LV00012B/2204

* 9 7 8 1 7 3 2 8 8 8 5 8 6 *